Nathan Crick

Loretta Pecchioni

Joni Butcher

DECONSTRUCTING COMMUNICATION

An Introduction to Rhetorical, Performance, and Communication Theory

Cover image courtesy of Tom Stoddart Archive/Getty Images.

BERLIN, GERMANY—November 10, 1989: A man offers a flower as a sign of peace to East German border guards on the morning that the first section of the Berlin Wall was pulled down.

Printed in the United States of America

10 9 8 7

ISBN 0-536-48881-9

2007560134

AG/SB

Please visit our web site at *www.pearsoncustom.com*

PEARSON CUSTOM PUBLISHING
501 Boylston Street, Suite 900, Boston, MA 02116
A Pearson Education Company

Contents

Introduction

To study communication is, in many ways, analogous to the old Indian fable about the blind men and the elephant. One man feels its leg and thinks the elephant is like a tree; one man touches its trunk and believes it is like a snake; and another man grabs its tusk and declares it is like a spear. Each offers a partial description of the animal but fails to grasp how the parts make up a whole. Communication is like the elephant if only for its sheer magnitude. Everything we do cooperatively in society (and often alone as well) implicates us in some communicative act, whether it is something obvious like a speech or something more subtle like a glance or a conspicuous silence. To try to offer a single, comprehensive description of communication often seems an insurmountable challenge.

As a result, we make sense of communication by using popular metaphors. We might think of communication, for instance, as a kind of data processing. We *network* to improve our connectivity, we *multitask* to improve productivity, or we *process* information to help us understand. Or maybe we think of communication as a game. Conversations are competitions and we all play by the rules to get ahead with the tools of wit and subterfuge. Both of these descriptions are partly true but also inadequate. To think we are just machines leaves out the emotional and symbolic nature of our interactions with other people. To see life as a game excludes those shared moments when we enjoy each other's company or make sacrifices for higher ends. Each of these metaphors reveals important aspects of communication but is incomplete on its own.

The academic study of communication is no different. To make it manageable, scholars specialize in different fields and develop unique terminologies that describe in detail specific aspects of communication. They all, in effect, choose their own part of the elephant. To study *rhetoric* means to focus on those messages that persuade public audiences to think or act in specific ways. Rhetoric calls to mind the study of oratory, when a person stands in front of a crowd and makes a formal speech to a waiting audience. To study *performance* means to see human behavior as a drama with actors, a scene, and a plot. We associate performance with those times when we are consciously playing roles, whether we are actors on a stage or children on the playground. And to study *communication theory* means, in broad terms, to understand messages are exchanged and meaning negotiated between two or more people. Communication in this sense happens constantly in everyday life whenever we say hello to a neighbor, talk at a business meeting, or speak with our family.

One way to think about the distinctions between rhetoric, performance, and communication theory is in terms of their relationship to *values*. Our values are core ideals about what we consider intrinsically right or wrong that show us how to conduct our lives. For rhetoric, values are resources to *draw from* and *use* when attempting to persuade a public audience. American politicians tend to sound the same, not necessarily because their policies are identical but because they employ the same values in defending their positions. How many times do you hear political speeches that justify legislative proposals on the basis of "freedom" and "liberty"? The reason for this tendency is the necessity for rhetorical discourse to adapt to the values of its audience and be an effective means of persuasion. In the United States, we are taught to value freedom and liberty as the hallmarks of democracy. Consequently, American audiences tend to listen only to those orators who "speak" our values. Like Martin Luther King Jr. did masterfully in his "I Have a Dream" speech, the most successful orations ground themselves in the values of their audience even when they are criticizing that audience for not living up to them. Rhetorical discourse connects with the basic values of an audience while simultaneously using it to encourage the adoption of new beliefs and attitudes.

In performance, the desire to simply be "heard" tends to outweigh the rhetorical demand to be followed or respected. Consequently, performances tend to *express* or *criticize* values for their own sake rather than use them for some instrumental end. In everyday life, simple choices of what to drive, wear, eat, or listen to often express some values that we hold dear. Do we drive a hybrid or a Humvee? Do we wear a suit or a T-shirt? Do we eat fast food or buy organic? Do we listen to classical music or hip hop? Everything we do in public life tends to associate us with the values of some community or group. Alternately, more artistic performances, such as avant-garde art, take these values and present them into more dramatic form in such a way that we can see our values differently. The documentary *Super Size Me* was a popular hit largely because it showed how the American value of cheap fast food has devastating health effects when taken to the extreme. Performances of this kind take our values and make us see them in a new light, thereby shining light on our world and ourselves.

Finally, communication theory tends to look at human interaction as a process of value *negotiation* and *choice*. In most of our conversations with others that are more than simply the exchange of pleasantries or the transmission of information, we involve ourselves in discussions that challenge us to define or choose between values. In other words, communication theory tends to focus on those moments when there is a moral conflict or dilemma in which people must use communication to come to a decision. Take, for instance, the cases of two parents trying to decide whether they should access their child's email to ensure its safety, employees confronting their boss about a discriminatory work environment, or a married couple arguing about whether to spend money on a lavish vacation. In each of these, there is a conflict between values—privacy or security, loyalty or equality, and frugality or pleasure. Or at times there is only one value at issue and the question is how to interpret it in practice. Am I loyal to a friend by standing by her decision even when I think she is wrong or by telling her the truth? Do I express love for someone by letting go or holding on? Is success determined by wealth or by happiness? Communication is the process by which we negotiate these meanings with others, and in our own minds, as we attempt to deal with the continual challenges we face throughout our lives.

The fields of rhetoric, performance, and communication theory each provides a unique way of interpreting human interaction, but one must always remember that they are only perspectives on a larger whole. From the above descriptions, one can already see the connections between the three areas. Just as an elephant can be examined equally by physics, chemistry, and biology, so can the process of communication be interpreted three different ways for three different purposes. In the end, however, our various interpretations should never be taken to stand in for what they interpret. After all the blind men's descriptions, there is still just the elephant. So too with communication.

Let us take three examples:

1. Every day you go to your favorite café to buy a coffee. Initially, you had trouble ordering correctly, being unfamiliar with all the new terminology required to get what you want from the barista. But after going there for several months you no longer even need to say anything. The barista sees you, nods, and simply starts making your order. You enjoy going to this particular café because it has outdoor tables facing the street and you like the "European" feel it gives you, especially after having recently read a novel about a writer living in Paris. You mention this once while making your order and the employee mentions that they

have a fancy new drink that uses Pernod, a version of a liqueur once favored by Parisian artists.

2. You go to hear a presidential candidate who comes to campus to give a stump speech. As you walk through the entrance gate they give you a campaign button which you see everyone else wearing. You don't know if you really like the candidate but you wear it anyway. When the candidate finally comes on stage he is dressed in a casual blue shirt with the sleeves rolled up, despite the fact that it is cold outside. Alongside him is a famous country singer who earlier did a song to rally the crowd. To your surprise, the candidate picks up the singer's guitar and the two of them sing a short song about being an American, which you think comes off rather silly. During his speech you also notice the candidate intentionally using slang phrases that you hear students using around campus.

3. For your anniversary you and your spouse go to the opera. You've never gone before and you buy a nice outfit for the occasion and try to read up on opera etiquette so as not to embarrass yourself. You are sitting in the front row and once the show starts you get cramped from trying to read the English subtitles that are being displayed above the stage. Eventually you give up and just try to enjoy the show. You are pleasantly surprised that you can follow the story without the subtitles due to the exaggerated actions of the players. You even begin to understand how the plot of the opera actually functions as a criticism of monarchy, which must have been very controversial when it was written, considering that the writer lived under that form of government.

All of these situations are complex events in which different facets of communication intertwine and overlap. To begin disentangling these facets one simply needs to ask some simple questions to direct our attention to details. When are verbal or nonverbal messages used for the purpose of generating a common meaning or facilitating cooperative action? In what ways can one describe any of the behaviors of individuals as actors in a drama or characters in a play? What actions are done to persuade people to alter or reinforce their attitudes or habits? After answering these questions, you will already begin to see how different perspectives direct attention to different details and make us understand each situation in a new and varied way.

The purpose of this course, then, is to introduce you to these three ways of looking at communication while emphasizing that each conveys only one perspective on a larger process. This course emphasizes not only differences in each perspective but also their similarities. In this case, the similarities are that each perspective on communication involves an *agent* who conveys a *message* to an *audience* that carries with it some *meaning*. The structure of the book is based on these four concepts. Rather than support the teaching of three "mini-courses" in rhetorical, performance, and communication theory, this book encourages the creative interplay between the discourses by explaining them through shared conceptual categories. By showing how each perspective defines and analyzes these categories, students will come away with a better idea of both the uniqueness of and the continuity between the different fields of communication. We hope that by doing so students can better adapt to the practical challenges that communication presents them once they leave the classroom.

History of the Disciplines of Communication

Each area of communication has its own unique history that determines its orientation and purpose. Understanding that history provides a better practical understanding of how and when to apply the conceptual tools specific to its theoretical perspective.

History of Rhetoric

Although rhetoric can loosely be defined as the art of *persuasion*, rhetorical theory is not simply the study of persuasion. To understand this distinction, one must appreciate the origins of rhetoric in the democratic age of classical Greece. Before the fifth century B.C., never had there existed a social system based on the principle that law should be written and interpreted by the citizenry rather than the powerful elite. In ancient Egypt, for instance, pharaohs were seen as gods and their decrees were identified with divine law. The stability of this social structure thus depended in large part on the ability of the ruling class to "persuade" the people to accept this hierarchy as the natural way of things. Accordingly, the pyramids were not simply private tombs but a form of public propaganda meant to inspire awe and reverence in the people. Today we see the manifestation of these same persuasive strategies in contemporary advertising, where giant billboards and flashy promotions strive to give brand names the same aura of mystery and power that once emanated from the pharaohs' golden masks. To study *persuasion* is thus to understand all the ways that people try to influence the beliefs and behaviors of others through symbolic manipulation and dissemination.

Rhetoric is undoubtedly a form of persuasion but it is one that reflects its democratic origins. In classical Greece, rulers and their decrees lost the divine sanction that propped up the pharaohs for centuries. Instead, responsibility for the creation and enforcement of law fell to the citizenry. While admittedly a limited citizenry by modern standards because it excluded women, slaves, and all those not born in the city-state, this public nonetheless was based on the modern principle that government should be run by the people and not by autocratic rulers. In practice this meant that citizens were responsible for both the making of laws as well as their adjudication in the law courts. Policies and judgments (in the ideal, at least) were to be determined on the strength of one's arguments rather than the level of one's social position.

The art of rhetoric emerged in this historical context as the means for social advocacy and judicial arbitration. It was, in this sense, not so much an art of *persuasion* as it was a *deliberative* art employed for the purposes of making collective judgments about public affairs. Rhetorical *theory* then described how rhetoric functioned in a democratic public sphere. It provided a framework for identifying the contexts in which rhetoric arose, describing the different genres of rhetoric appropriate for those contexts, showing the strategies that rhetoric employed to address its audiences, and judging how rhetoric facilitated or inhibited the growth of democratic society.

Theorists were by no means uniform on their judgments of rhetoric. For the sophists, who earned money teaching the art of rhetoric to those willing to pay, democracy was strongest when rhetoric flourished. They were generally skeptical of the received "truths" of tradition and instead put their faith in whatever conclusions were reached after the clash of rhetorical competition in the public sphere. By contrast, aristocrats like Plato saw the proliferation of rhetoric much as we now see the ubiquity of advertising—as a sign of decadence and decline. He wanted to control rhetoric by making it only a tool for spreading Truth, Beauty, and Goodness while banning all discourse that failed to reach that level. Reaching a compromise was Aristotle, who believed that rhetoric was useful in limited contexts of uncertainty and crisis where we had to make decisions without definitive sciences to guide us. Where precise knowledge is available, said Aristotle, rhetoric is unnecessary. But when our path ahead is unclear, rhetorical deliberation allows for the possibility that truth can be heard, recognized, and understood by the common public. In this sense, we do not debate publicly about how to build a bridge, but we do debate about where to build it; we don't argue about how to do a heart transplant, but we do argue about who should receive a heart; and we don't question how to predict a hurricane, but we do question how to best distribute resources after its landfall.

For the purposes of this book, we will largely follow the Aristotelian interpretation by defining rhetoric as *the art of using persuasive discourse as a means of addressing public problems before public audiences.* Ironically, however, "rhetoric" as it is commonly used today tends to reflect the Platonic definition. Rather than seeing rhetoric as a tool for making intelligent collective judgments, we often accuse politicians of engaging in "mere rhetoric" when they should be telling the truth and getting things done. Undoubtedly, political discourse often fits this interpretation. However, to align "rhetoric" with "empty words" is to invert the original meaning of the term. Rhetoric in classical Greece was not just a way of talking pretty; it was an instrument of action. In this sense, the highest examples of rhetoric in American history include artifacts like the Gettysburg Address, the Declaration of Independence, and the Federalist Papers, just as the best rhetors include citizens like Thomas Paine, Susan B. Anthony, and Frederick Douglass.

Most of us cannot expect to attain such rhetorical heights. However, democracy is based on the faith that our collective rhetorical achievements, however small in their particularity, will constitute a society in which law and convention both express the popular will and ensure the rights of individuals. We participate in this process whenever we stand up for what we believe in the public sphere and use our critical skills to judge the words of others who do the same. As in classical Greece, learning the art of rhetoric is to do more than learn how to persuade people to do what you want them to do; it is to learn how to make your voice heard, understand critically what you hear from others, and thereby participate in the democratic process.

History of Performance

Many wonder why performance is included as part of the field of communication. The word *communication* itself means "to make common," or "to share information and ideas." Communication involves social interaction in which messages are shared, transmitted, or exchanged. Performance is a way of sharing, transmitting, and exchanging messages between performers and the audience. Although the area of performance has common ties with both theatrical and rhetorical traditions, the history of performance can be traced through three major movements: 1) the origins of oral poetry and oral traditions, 2) the emergence of oral interpretation and interpreters theatre, and 3) the shift from oral interpretation to performance studies.

Oral Poetry and Oral Traditions

Performers have always been storytellers. Early performers were song-stitchers who sewed together various poetic episodes into continuous, connected stories. These oral poets served as both historians and entertainers. The stories they told, or sang, helped maintain historical records of their villages and tribes, or reaffirmed social values by stressing the power of love, the magnificence of heroic deeds, or the pure pleasure of engaging in the art of storytelling.

One such group of storytellers, the *rhapsodes,* existed in fourth and fifth century Greece, where they traveled from town to town performing epic poetry. They wore signature cloaks and carried a staff which signified their right or power to tell their stories. Many rhapsodes performed at religious festivals where they competed against each other for prizes and recognition as master storytellers. A second group, the Anglo-Saxon *scops*, performed Old English ballads which praised kings or recounted heroic battles. Scops usually recited or sang their stories while accompanying themselves on harps or other stringed instruments. A third group of storytellers, the French *troubadours*, were poet-musicians who performed across Europe during the 11th century. Many traveled for great distances spreading their songs of chivalry and courtly love. They often engaged in poetic debates where one troubadour would deliver a question or message in song and it was answered or refuted via the song of another troubadour.

In addition to the art of storytelling, the study of voice and gesture greatly influenced the area of performance during the 19th century. During this period in history, Americans were becoming increasingly interested in science. Scientific technology gave individuals more power over their environment and allowed for more leisure time. Science was also used to critique art. Performance theorists at the time believed the more scientifically knowledgeable one became, the more one's artistic consciousness was raised. Thus, better science leads to better art. Two groups, the *elocutionists* and the *expressionists*, viewed the body as a machine. These theorists advocated a triangular relationship between science, speaking skills, and performance. Scientific principles could be used to improve speaking skills, and better speaking skills would lead to more refined performances.

Elocutionists of the *mechanical school* believed that in order to be an effective "reader," each word of the text needed to carry a specific intonation. Readers, or interpreters, memorized these intonations and then repeated them when reciting their texts. Elocutionists of the *natural school*, on the other hand, believed that words should be more conversational in style. The term *natural*, however, is a bit misleading since the theorists of the natural school had specific guidelines for how to accomplish a natural, conversational tone.

The *expressionists* were similar to the elocutionists, but they carried interpretation a step further by incorporating mind, gesture, and expression into the recitations. Expressionists believed that the performer should become "one" with the poem, and thereby edify the soul through the interpretation. But once again, the body was treated as a machine. Gestures and expressions were calculated as an exact science. Elaborate diagrams were drawn to show the performer the exact arm positions and facial expression for each emotion.

Oral Interpretation and Intepreters Theatre

The discipline of *oral interpretation* emerged in the early 1940s. Oral interpretation concentrated on reading texts aloud and with feeling. The focus was on a *presentational* mode of performance in which voice, gesture, body movement, and facial expression were used to create symbolic imagery that would evoke an imaginative response on the part of the audience. For example, a simple nod of the head could be used to signify a complete bow or a few steps could indicate a long walk. The text was the primary emphasis with the performers serving to illuminate the text for the audience. Interpreters Theatre consisted of both *Readers Theatre* and *Chamber Theatre,* which still survive today as methods of performance.

In *Readers Theatre*, performers, usually dressed in white shirts and black pants or skirts, read texts aloud while seated on stools behind music stands or lecterns. There is almost no use of sets, lights, costumes, makeup, or physical movement. The entire cast remains onstage throughout the performance. Their purpose is to illuminate the text for the audience. Readers Theatre works best with texts that are rich in language and auditory appeals since the focus is on language instead of action.

Chamber Theatre was developed by Robert Breen as a technique for staging narrative literature. Breen disapproved of the practice of making stories "dramatic" by eliminating the presence of the storyteller. He wanted the audience to experience watching a story as opposed to viewing a dramatic play, so Breen decided to stage these works by leaving the narrative element intact. Thus, Chamber Theatre productions incorporate a narrator who speaks, or tells the story, to the audience, as well as characters who bring the story to life. While Readers Theatre uses only the presentational mode of performance, Chamber Theatre combines elements of both the presentational and representational modes. Minimal costuming, set pieces and props are used, and performers make use of the stage space as a container for action. Thus, while Readers Theatre focuses on *telling*, Chamber Theatre incorporates both *telling* and *showing*.

Performance Studies

Beginning in the 1980s, the area of performance began to branch out from the oral interpretation of poetry and narrative literature. Literary texts were still studied and performed, but scholars and practitioners expanded their focus to cultural texts as well. Life, culture, and art were viewed as viable areas of performance. The idea of performance in everyday life, for example, became a field for investigation. Performers observed how we alter our actions, behaviors, dialogue, and physical appearance to take on roles in our everyday surroundings. In addition to everyday life performance, performance scholars explored performative behaviors within communities. They studied performative elements in such cultural events as weddings, festivals, football games, and parades. Finally, many postmodern or avant-garde performers explored performance as an element of social change. They examined, for example, how a work of performance art can challenge the established social, cultural, or political order through shock, provocation, or disturbance.

Thus, from the 1980s to the present day, the area of performance is known as performance studies instead of oral interpretation. Though the performance of literary texts is certainly included in today's performance arena, the field has expanded to embrace numerous other performance texts.

History of Communication Theory

Communication theory is the area of communication studies that focuses on identifying how individuals and groups exchange and assign meaning to messages. The history of communication theory is driven by the desire to apply scientific methods to understanding these social processes. In order to understand the historical development of communication theory, it is helpful to understand the overarching assumptions held by communication theorists about how the social world works. Three interrelated assumptions about the nature of humans and the role of communication in our lives are basic to the research conducted by communication theorists: 1) the world is a relatively predictable place; 2) humans make sense of their experiences; and, 3) we make and follow rules with regards to our social interactions.

Assumptions of Communication Theory

Predictability. Babies learn, hopefully, that when they cry, someone comes and tends to their needs. This process leads to a basic understanding of cause and effect—when one thing happens, another thing follows as a result of the first thing happening. As we develop a broader understanding of the relationship between cause and effect, we develop a sense of mastery and control over our world. Humans tend to prefer some level of predictability. For example, when we put the key in the ignition of our car, we expect the car to start and are frustrated when it doesn't, especially if we're running late to class or an important meeting! Human behavior is not as predictable as mechanical behavior. We do, however, have expectations about what will happen in social situations. We expect that if we work hard, we will be rewarded accordingly. If we are kind to other people, we expect them to be kind in return. If we share personal information, we expect others to do the same. Over our lives, we make observations about things that happen, see patterns, and make predictions about these events.

Sense-making. The cognitive activity related to observing the world, seeing patterns and making predictions about human behavior is part of our sense-making ability. Our brains actively process and organize information so that we can later access and use that information. Our brains, however, are not simply data storage devices. They are also meaning-making devices. For example, if someone you know well is acting "strangely," then you will try to understand what is making him or her act in ways that are not typical of him or her. In order for this situation to occur, you must first have some sense of what is normal behavior for your friend so that you come to the conclusion that his or her behavior is "strange." Then you might think of things that could have happened that would cause him or her to act in this unusual manner. The process of reconciling this unusual behavior with your typical expectations for this friend is part of the sense-making process.

Rules. Humans do not always act in predictable ways, but we do tend to be rule makers and followers. The social groups to which we belong make rules that indicate appropriate behavior in different settings. For example, in the United States, we drive on the right side of the road (a legal rule, we can get a ticket for doing otherwise). Other rules are not necessarily laws and have less stringent consequences if the rule is violated. While we are required to drive on the right side of the road, do we have to walk down a crowded hallway on the right side? What happens when we don't?

As a child, we start to pick up rules by observing others, but we also receive explicit instructions regarding how to behave properly in a given situation. For example, we are likely to get specific instructions from our parents or other caregivers about how to behave in school or at our place of worship. Other rules for behavior may not receive such explicit instruction. For example, we have rules about what it means to be a friend, even if we haven't thought about what they are.

In spite of being rule makers and followers, we sometimes violate the rules of our social groups. The outcomes for such violations may be negative or positive. For example, the general rule in elevators is to face the doors and evenly distribute ourselves throughout the space. If you enter an elevator with one other person, what happens if you stand right next to that person? Usually, that rule violation will cause the other person to move away from you in order to create the "appropriate" amount of space between you. However, sometimes this rule violation might have a positive outcome. What if the person on the elevator is someone that you know slightly and you are hoping to get to know that person better? Maybe that person also wants to get to know you better. If so, your rule violation may open up discussion between the two of you so that you start to develop a relationship.

Developing Communication Theory

Communication theory scholars are interested in uncovering the rules of behavior that different groups hold in order to understand those rules and to make predictions about what people will do and what happens if they violate those rules. Often, communication theory scholars talk about prediction and control. I want to predict what someone else is likely do in a situation so that I can establish some control over our interaction.

With the focus of the assumptions of prediction, sense-making, and rules, communication theorists often adopt a scientific approach to their research. Development of this perspective on communication is usually attributed to a group of researchers who were concerned about propaganda around the time of World War II in the 1940s. They wanted to understand the power of messages, not from the perspective of rhetoric by focusing on the language choices made to create an appealing message, but rather by applying scientific principles to discover how people interpret messages and take action. They wanted to be able to predict and control the impact of messages by understanding what motivated people. In this process, they conducted experiments in which they manipulated the credibility of the speaker and asked people to report how they would respond to a persuasive argument. As a result, they learned what characteristics lead to greater credibility and the best ways to present those characteristics to the audience in order to get the desired response from the audience.

In the United States, communication theory took a turn during the 1960s and 70s from a focus on the public forum to more personal communication exchanges. This era saw considerable social upheaval with groups protesting the Vietnam War, the civil rights movement, and the women's movement. Each of these groups had in common the desire to have people's voices heard more effectively and to change the social structure. While the status quo regarding relationships between social groups was being challenged, the nature of interpersonal relationships was also being redefined. Instead of the norm of acting toward each other based on scripted ways of interacting, people were encouraged to "really get to know each other," therefore they had to negotiate the rules of their particular relationships and to interact in ways that reflected personal preferences rather than socially prescribed behaviors.

The scientific approach used by communication theorists argues that in order to understand human behavior, we should develop and test theories that not only explain communicative behavior, but also predict what will happen. A basic underlying tenet of communication theory is that communication is the process by which we negotiate meaning with others, and in our own minds, as we attempt to deal with the continual challenges we face throughout our lives. This view of communication is based on two prominent theories: *symbolic interaction* and the *social construction of reality*.

Symbolic interaction focuses on how the individual and society are interrelated. As we discuss throughout this text, symbols are used to exchange information. However, the meaning of any symbol must be agreed upon by a social group and that meaning is often fluid. As children, we are socialized into our primary social group. We learn not just the language, but the values and rituals that are important to our primary social group, generally our family of origin. As we develop language, we learn how to label concrete things (e.g., "ball," "mama") and then more abstract ideas (e.g., "honesty," "pride"). The important people around you guide your behavior by providing feedback on whether you are getting it "right" or "wrong." As you learn these lessons, you internalize them so that you no longer need feedback from others to "know" how you value a certain behavior. As a result, you begin to think of yourself in certain ways and you act in ways that are consistent with a desired view of yourself.

Because social groups assign meaning to symbols, how we view the world depends on our social groups. The social construction of reality means just that—we learn to see the world in certain ways because we jointly create meaning with those around us. The meanings assigned to symbols change across individuals and social groups. For example, when you think of the word "dog," English speakers generally agree that this symbol represents a particular kind of animal. However, different people may picture different dogs in their minds when they hear or see the word "dog." You may picture a particular dog that is or was a family pet, or one that bit you when you were a child. For some individuals, dogs are considered to be like family members while others think of them as work animals. Some social groups think of dogs as a meat source whereas other social groups find that thought repellent. Because the meaning assigned to symbols is jointly created, different groups often have different perspectives on the meaning assigned to a symbol. One goal for the communication theorist is to examine how symbols come to have unique or idiosyncratic meaning while at the same time having shared meaning (at least within a social group that sees the world in similar ways). In this view of communication, we *live in* communication. That is, communication is not just a tool for conveying information, but influences what we see, think, and feel about objects in our world and we use communication to negotiate meaning.

The more scientific approach used by communication theorists in combination with the assumption that communication is a complex process has led to the idea that in order to examine any facet of communication, other facets have to eliminated or controlled. As a result, communication theorists often focus on a particular context. Many factors influence what behaviors will be deemed appropriate in a given setting. Because communication scholars have a desire to be able to identify patterns of behavior and to predict people's actions, they often limit the focus of communication to some context that attempts to control the number of factors being studied at any given point in time. Ordinary people do not usually label these contexts, but they do adapt their behavior to the situation. For communication theorists, the contexts usually considered are based on the situation, especially how many people are involved and whether they are face-to-face or interacting through a mediated format. Typically, these contexts are called: intrapersonal, interpersonal, group, organizational, public, and mass communication.

Intrapersonal communication focuses on the individual and cognitive processing. Your attitudes influence how you process information and the meaning that you assign to a message. For example, if you generally dislike loud people because you think they are rude, when you meet someone who is loud, you will also assume that he or she is rude and will probably avoid further interaction.

Interpersonal communication focuses on two people interacting (usually) face-to-face, who are in some kind of relationship with one another, such as friends, romantic partners, family members, or coworkers. Much of the research in this area examines how we develop and maintain relationships, how different styles of relationships are revealed by and through communication, and how relational partners negotiate meeting multiple goals in their interactions. While much of the research on interpersonal communication focuses on face-to-face interaction, a growing area of interest is how new media (the Internet, cell phones, etc.) impact the development and maintenance of personal and social relationships.

Group communication focuses on small groups who are interacting in order to accomplish a joint goal. These groups are usually in some kind of an organizational setting. Much of the research in this area focuses on how organizational members make decisions and what communicative behaviors lead to better decision-making by the group. While these groups have an instrumental task (a specific goal to accomplish), the social aspects of the group may take precedence in understanding the dynamics of the group.

Organizational communication focuses on the communication that occurs in formal organizations, such as businesses or governmental agencies. Communication in organizations may be interpersonal, such as coworkers talking, but communication scholars also examine how communication reveals and creates the culture of an organization. Because of the formal nature of these relationships, how power is used or displayed is often an important issue of research by communication theorists.

Public communication focuses on those events when one person is speaking to many others and is closely related to rhetoric. While rhetoric focuses on the art of persuasion in the context of public deliberation over matters of controversy, communication theorists studying public communication examine the science of persuasion as it relates to constructing a particular persuasive text for a specific instrumental end. They ask such questions as: What makes a source seem credible? What channels of communication are most likely to reach a desired audience? What messages would be most effective in leading an audience to take action with regard to an issue?

Mass communication focuses on mediated communication, usually when one person or a small group of people are developing content that will be shared with a large group of consumers, specifically the traditional media—television, radio, newspapers and magazines. As the Internet has changed who can place content in a public forum or how two people meet and get to know each other, this area is undergoing considerable change.

For this class, we will focus primarily on interpersonal communication and the social groups that help us to define what we think is appropriate communication.

In sum, *communication theory* attempts to understand how messages are exchanged and meaning is negotiated between two or more people. Communication theorists believe that what we say and do create our relationships and define who we are as individuals. If we return to the core concept of values as discussed in the introduction to this text, we can see how human interaction reveals the processes of value *negotiation* and *choice*. Let's examine one of the examples from the introduction in more detail. A friend asks your opinion about an important matter. What does it mean to be a good friend? Do you tell her what you honestly think, even if you don't believe that she wants to hear it? Do you tell her you think she would be making a mistake, but you will support her no matter what she does? Do you ignore her problem and tell her about your own crisis, even though it is relatively minor? Your choices reveal what you think it means to be a good friend, what you value in your relationship with this person, and how you want to be seen by others.

Section 1

Agent

The agent in communication refers generally to the individual who initiates a communicative act.

The Agent In Communication Theory

From the perspective of communication theory, the ***agent*** is the individual who is speaking, writing, or behaving in meaningful ways. The individual is viewed as continuously being "in dialogue." That dialogue occurs within the individual's mind or in conversation with others. We are continually making sense of the world and sharing the sense we make with others. In communication theory, then, we tend to focus on the *action* of communicating, i.e., making sense of our world, playing our roles, and developing our sense of self as we present that self to others.

While communication theorists often focus on an individual's behavior, we always note that communication is transactional—the agent and the audience are attempting to build shared understanding. Therefore, the agent and the audience share responsibility for the conversation and both are actively involved in the creation of the interaction. As a consequence, it is difficult to completely separate the agent from the audience because we are simultaneously both in conversation. As a person is talking, he or she is also paying attention to the other person to see how that person is responding while also trying to understand what the other person means. Think about a time when you were telling a friend about an event. How did your friend indicate that he or she understood or did not understand what you were talking about? Did your friend ask specific questions or get a puzzled look on his or her face? You were both engaged in making sense out of the messages that you were exchanging.

In communication theory, we focus particularly on certain elements of the agent—perception, roles, and the self—and how those elements are created and impact our behaviors. An individual takes in stimuli, organizes those stimuli into patterns and interprets those patterns. How we organize stimuli impacts the roles that we take up in our lives and our sense of self and these in turn impact how we organize stimuli.

Perception

We are bombarded with stimuli. What do you see, hear, feel, taste, and smell, this moment? Are you aware of your clothes on your skin? The pressure of your chair? Is that song that's playing drawing your attention away from your reading? The number of sensations that we can pay attention to at any given moment is limited, so we become selective about what receives our attention. ***Perception***, then, is the active process of selecting certain stimuli from the wide array of stimuli we are receiving and creating patterns and making sense out of those patterns. You learn not to pay attention to the feel of your clothes on your skin, unless you have a sunburn or a rash. You don't pay attention to these constant stimuli, but focus your attention on other stimuli.

This *selection* process consists of paying attention to certain stimuli while ignoring others. This process becomes so automatic that we aren't even aware that we are ignoring the majority of signals being sent to our brains. In addition, we quickly move to interpreting stimuli. Organizing and interpreting stimuli is almost instantaneous with their reception. *Organizing stimuli* is the process of creating categories and assigning stimuli to those categories. Humans inherently seek patterns. As infants we begin to organize stimuli into categories. These categories make life much easier for us. We don't have to pay attention to everything all the time and we don't have to figure out everything anew each time we encounter a stimulus. We develop mental structures to help us quickly place people, places, things, and events into categories and to apply the appropriate rules for behavior.

Interpreting stimuli is the process of assigning meaning based on the categories to which they are assigned. When we are interacting with other people, we observe their behavior and then not only assign a label to that behavior, but also draw inferences about their motives, personalities, and other traits. When you see someone walking quickly across campus, do you think "she's in a hurry, she must be late for class," or do you think "she must have grown up some place where people are always on the move"? Two people watching the same scene will not interpret it in exactly the same way. You assign meaning to her brisk pace based on your experiences and attitudes as well as the setting.

Organizing and interpreting stimuli develops a set of cognitive structures. These *cognitive structures* are mental structures that help us rapidly assess an object, thing, person, or event and determine a set of expectations in relation to its category. These mental structures filter what we pay attention to, the meaning that we assignto it, and how we react in response.

Roles

When you ask the question—"Who am I?,"—one of the ways you answer that question is by listing the roles that you play ("I'm a student, daughter, friend, volunteer, etc."). A ***role*** is a set of expected behaviors that are associated with a particular situation and guide how we are expected to behave toward others. We play multiple roles and these roles may even be in conflict with each other. For example, sometimes the roles of being a good student and being a good employee collide due to time demands.

As social creatures, our roles are often defined in conjunction with the roles of others—parent-child, husband-wife, boss-employee, student-teacher, etc. When we play our part as expected, not only do others think well of us, but we derive satisfaction from "a job well done." Successfully playing a role can make us feel better about ourselves while feeling like we failed in playing our part can make us feel bad about ourselves.

When interacting with others, the roles that we are playing become important in managing our interactions successfully. Who we are and how we want others to see us impacts impression formation and management. *Impressions* are collections of perceptions that we use to interpret behavior, whether that behavior is our own or others'. Generally, we want other people to like us, think we're competent and capable, or some other characteristic that we value in a particular setting. Therefore, we choose to reveal certain aspects of ourselves to others in the hopes that they will judge us as we want to be judged. Basically, we develop *identity scripts* that guide us in how to behave so that others will judge us in certain ways. For example, we may have identity scripts for what it means to be a good daughter, a good student, a good employee, etc. Depending on the behaviors we associate with each script and the setting, we choose to act in ways that demonstrate we know the script. One of the main goals of identity management is to avoid embarrassment, shame, or humiliation.

The Self

While a role is a set of expected behaviors that are associated with a particular situation, the self is a broader concept. When most people ask themselves, "Who am I?," they not only list the various roles that they fill, but also personality traits, and what they like and don't like about themselves. One person might respond to that question: "I'm a student, daughter, friend, I'm honest and hard-working, organized and focused, but sometimes, I'm too rigid." The *self* is the evolving composite of our traits, roles, attitudes, and experiences and our evaluation of how we feel about those elements. Your sense of self, however, may grow out of how you manage your multiple roles by determining "who" you are as you identify what you like and dislike about how you play your roles. One of the processes of life is to continually make some kind of coherent sense of how all these elements fit together, especially when we are challenged by new experiences. This process depends on reflection and assessing how we feel about who we are.

As we discussed in the introduction to communication theory, symbolic interaction argues that we develop our sense of who we are through our interactions with others. We learn how others see us and we internalize their view into our view of ourselves. We then think about who we are and whether we like what we learn about ourselves. *Self-awareness* is the ability to look at your self as a unique individual and to reflect on your feelings, thoughts, and behaviors. Through self-awareness, you develop your *self-concept*, that is, your overall cognitive image of who you are, based on your beliefs, attitudes, and values. You also evaluate whether or not you like what you see in your self. *Self-esteem* is the value you place on your self, that is, whether you like or dislike who you are. Of course, it is quite possible to like certain aspects of who you are and to dislike other aspects. For example, if you have a set of expectations about what it means to be a good daughter, but you don't live up to those expectations, you are likely to feel bad about yourself. Through self-awareness, you reflect on your behaviors. You identify that your behaviors are not aligned with your values, so you feel that you have not lived up to the self-concept you have of yourself. Because you feel bad about your behavior, your self-esteem is lowered. In order to improve your self-esteem, you may vow to change your behavior so that it is aligned with your expectations for your behavior.

An important aspect of the self is the nature of the public versus the private self. The *public self* is what others know about us, while the *private self* is the part of us that we keep to ourselves. These elements of the self exist on a continuum from public to private. When you meet someone face-to-face, you make certain assumptions about that person based on physical characteristics, such as sex, ethnicity, and age. You don't know, however, how that person feels about his or her sex, ethnicity, and age. Through our interactions with others, we share information about ourselves (that is, our traits, roles, attitudes, and experiences and our evaluation of how we feel about those elements). As social creatures, we attempt to manage some level of publicly shared and privately held information. We will talk more about public and private selves when we talk about social and personal relationships and the impact they have on communicative behavior. For now, it is important to think about what we choose to reveal to others about who we "really" are. Through self-awareness, we know what we don't like about ourselves and we are less likely to share those aspects with others. On the other hand, we want others to think of us in certain ways, so we act in ways to encourage that view. These public selves reflect desired roles that we have taken up and that we want to portray to others. We often desire to display different public selves to different audiences. For example, we may want our friends to think of us one way and our parents another. With the accessibility of digital media, however, the line between public and private has become blurred and control over our private selves may be more difficult. Do you know anyone who has posted a video on his or her MySpace or Facebook page and then been embarrassed when his or her parent or employer saw the video?

The Agent in Rhetoric

The *agent* of rhetorical discourse is called a *rhetor*. A **rhetor** *is a conscious instigator of social action.* By *conscious* we mean that a rhetor has specific interests and goals and intentionally makes use of persuasion to achieve these goals. By *instigator* we mean a person whose actions cause others to think and feel in new and different ways. And by *social action* we mean that the effects of a rhetor's discourse are determined by how they impact the behaviors of other people with respect to some public issue. Defining the agent of rhetorical discourse is thus a process of identifying the relationship between a rhetor and his or her audience, establishing their commonalities and differences, and determining the productive consequences of their interaction.

Ethos

In Greek, the word for "character" is *ethos*. To have *ethos*, one has to possess three things: *virtue, practical wisdom*, and *good will*. That is to say, a person with character upholds the virtues we hold dear (honesty, courage, justice, and the like), has a history of making wise decisions that resolve problematic situations, and expresses a genuine concern for the well-being of others. For the ancient Greeks, character is something very "public"; it is a relative concept established on the basis of our outward behavior and productive achievements rather than a reflection of a private inner self. The concept of *ethos* thus has distinctly rhetorical implications in that it directly influences the level of trust we place in certain speakers when they address important decisions. Because we often do not have the time or resources to be able to make crucial judgments on our own, we look to those who possess strength of character to help guide our actions.

In politics, the importance of proving one's *ethos* is most in evidence by the ubiquity of attack ads intent on destroying the character of one's opponent. Although it is a constant refrain that negative ads of this kind debase the political process, the reality is that more often than not we vote for our leaders on the basis of character. In consumer culture, this principle is manifested in the use of celebrity spokespeople whose *ethos* is then transferred to a product. While there may be no logical connection between an actor and a sports car, there certainly is a persuasive connection to an audience who trusts the actor and knows nothing about the car.

The beginning of any rhetorical act must then start with an analysis of the character of the rhetor *relative* to the social environment in which he or she is speaking. That is to say, character in the rhetorical sense is not something absolute and stable that one carries around wherever one goes. *Ethos* is determined by the relationship one has to an audience. The president of a country may possess great *ethos* with respect to his or her own constituency and yet be despised by a foreign population. This is because any act can be interpreted differently by different groups. A Presidential declaration of war may be seen as a courageous defense of freedom by one side and a brutal act of imperialism by the other. To understand the possible effects of one's rhetoric, then, a person must understand the status of his or her public character within the audiences one addresses. This is determined by the relationship between the *nature* of their public acts and how those actions have been *interpreted* by a particular group, community, or society.

Persona

In contrast to *ethos*, the concept of *persona* relates not to the *actual* character or reputation of a speaker, but more narrowly to how a rhetor constructs and presents an image of himself or herself within a particular rhetorical text. Persona, in other words, is literally a creation of language; it is a "fiction" that the speaker wishes an audience to accept as real. Like the costume that transforms an actor into a new personality on stage, rhetoric can create a "public face" that best suits the immediate needs of a rhetor. Unlike *ethos*, which refers to the reputation one acquires through cumulative actions over time, one's persona is always tied to a specific discourse and is completely contained within that discourse. Consequently, one can interpret the persona that a rhetor creates within a rhetorical text without knowing anything about the "real" person who exists outside of that text. However, the intended function of a rhetorical persona is almost identical to that of *ethos*; it is to establish credibility with an audience and make oneself out to be a person whose words are worthy of hearing. The difference is that *ethos* is a result of actions and interactions with actual people and situations; persona is purely an "image."

Deciding when to construct a persona and when to rely on the strength of one's actual ethos is contingent upon the presence and quality of one's reputation with an audience. On the one hand, when a speaker is unknown to an audience, creating a persona is necessary in order to present a favorable "first impression." We are all familiar with those first-job interviews when we must define ourselves as an ideal employee (usually being careful to downplay or ignore the times when we have been less than ideal). On the other hand, when a speaker enters a situation as a respected leader, there is no need for such self-promotion; indeed, it would be seen in bad taste. Rarely do we enjoy listening to the famous and powerful bragging about their fame and power. Their ethos does the job for them. In-between these two extremes are more complex situations when a rhetor addresses a skeptical or hostile audience. In these cases one must construct a persona that somehow addresses and modifies one's inherited ethos. Celebrities caught up in embarrassing personal scandals often spend considerable time on talk shows attempting to shore up their ethos through repeated attempts to present a persona of one who is both ashamed of their actions and redeemed through their *mea culpas*. The strategy is usually to show how certain unpopular actions or expressions were aberrations or exceptions to their "true" self, which they then proceed to explain by constructing a persona.

Analysis of persona proceeds first through an isolated interpretation of a particular text, second by examining how it generates or modifies a rhetor's ethos, and third by an interpretation of how it influences an audience to accept or reject a rhetor's message. For example, let us take a teenage boy who has many times gotten into trouble at school and says to his father: "I've been a good son and have listened to you and all my life. So you can trust me with the car tonight." First, if one looks just at the words (the "text"), one sees the persona of a loyal and obedient son. Second, this persona is clearly in conflict with his established ethos, which is that of a troublemaker. Depending on the audience, this could have either positive or negative effects. Third, given the fact that the audience is his father, the attempt to gloss over previous poor behavior, thus showing a lack of character and responsibility in itself, will likely have the effect of making his father even less willing to lend him the car.

Interests

In rhetorical discourse, *interests* represent goals or purposes that require the agency of others to bring into being. In this sense, they are not simply likes or dislikes in the form of personal opinions. They are those likes or dislikes that a person has an *interest* in promoting and putting into action and that require cooperation from an audience to do so. For instance, a fondness for going to the beach is a *personal* interest. One can do this independently of others and satisfy some personal desire. However, when my individual habits are interrupted by the discovery of used hospital needles washing up on my favorite beach, this personal desire turns into a public passion to advocate for environmental regulation to ensure clean shorelines. Because this goal now requires support from a public audience and cooperation by administrative officials, this interest now becomes a *rhetorical* interest. Understanding any rhetorical act must, then, understand the public issues and goals toward which it is directed.

However, the interests that "truly" lie behind rhetorical discourse can often be hard to discern. This is because their interests can be *explicit* or *hidden*. *Explicit* interests are those interests which are clearly present in a rhetor's discourse. They usually take the form of *should* and *ought* statements, as in "We should implement environmental safeguards" and "we ought to protect our shoreline." *Hidden* interests are those interests which the rhetor possesses but which he or she does not make public. Hence, they are more difficult to determine because they are not stated in the text. Sometimes interests are hidden simply because listing them takes too much time, risk stating the obvious, or gets in the way of eloquence. The Chinese citizen who stood in front of the tanks at Tiananmen Square hardly needed to state his interests in doing so; his sheer presence made it obvious. However, often the purpose of hiding one's interests is for less honorable reasons, such as the fact that they may conflict with the interests of the audience, thereby inhibiting the ability to persuade. We often associate hidden interests of this sort with *propaganda* because we are not told the "full story," but only that part of the story that benefits the propagandist. Indeed, often times the hidden interests of propaganda directly contradict the explicit interests contained in the message! George Orwell's famous novel *1984* is based on this principle of what has come to be known as "Doublespeak." Hence, the "Ministry of Truth" spreads lies and the "Ministry of Peace" commits itself to an eternal state of war.

Definitively knowing the nature of a rhetor's hidden interests usually requires extensive research into the private documents of that rhetor, the kind of which are usually revealed by biographers who attempt to find out what world leaders were "truly" thinking during times of crisis. In most cases, however, the difficulty if not impossibility of ever determining such interests usually leaves their determination a matter of speculation and opinion. It is thus important to maintain a critical spirit when listening to any rhetorical discourse in the understanding that all rhetorical interests are rarely made explicit. It is to our benefit to develop when possible the critical skills to make a reasoned judgment concerning those interests which remain hidden even when we do not have concrete evidence with which to work.

Constraints

If we lived in a fantasy world, nothing would impede us from attaining our interests. Our wishes would be commands, and all impediments to our success would vanish from view. Of course, we do not live in a fantasy but in reality, where more often than not even our most mundane interests, like going to the store to buy bread, are obstructed by traffic jams, lack of transportation, or even our own forgetfulness. These obstacles that stand between us and the attainment of our interests are called *constraints*, in the sense of being something that restrains or inhibits movement.

Rhetorical constraints are those obstacles that must be overcome in order to facilitate both the persuasive and practical effects desired by the rhetor. There are, accordingly, two kinds of rhetorical constraints that correspond to the two kinds of effects. *Internal constraints* are the beliefs, attitudes, and values of an audience that must be changed if persuasion is to occur. For example, convincing a population to support a new spending project usually requires overcoming the skeptical attitudes of the public concerning the efficiency of government programs. Unless this internal constraint can be modified, then it will stand in the way of implementation.

External constraints are the objects, processes, and events that may physically obstruct any productive action even if persuasion of an audience has occurred. For example, if that spending project involves the building of a new rail transit system, external constraints might be the hills that surround a city that must be tunneled through (object), the federal bureaucracy that must approve the project (process), or the recent earthquake that disrupted the already existing railways (event). Any of these external constraints may impede successful social action even after an audience has been persuaded to act.

Successful rhetors always consider all possible constraints before creating and delivering rhetorical discourse. Ignoring constraints often ruins any possibility of instigating effective social action. On the one hand, if external constraints are ignored, then a rhetor risks appearing ignorant or simply overly idealistic concerning the "realities" of the situation. We often associate these kinds of speakers with poets and dreamers. On the other hand, ignoring internal constraints is the common flaw of all "technical" discourse that believes that the only thing needed for persuasion is accurate facts and reasonable solutions. We often associate these kinds of speakers with scientists and bureaucrats. The most effect rhetor combines elements of both types of discourse by adapting language to both types of constraint.

The Agent in Performance

In the area of performance, the agent is most commonly referred to as the *performer*. The performer can be described as the individual who creates messages or makes meaning via an aesthetically heightened form of communication. The performer's role may differ somewhat depending upon the type of performance in which the performer is engaged. Performance of everyday life, traditional literary performance, and nontraditional or alternative performance styles all influence the way the performer acts and is perceived by the audience.

Performance of Everyday Life

In performance of everyday life, the performer becomes a *role-taker* and *role-player*. As individuals, we all have a variety of roles that we enact in our everyday environments. One may play the role of a student during class time, the role of a salesclerk at an after-school job, and the role of a Sunday school teacher on the weekends. In each of these roles, the performer must create and express certain actions, behaviors, dialogues, and even costuming elements to enact the part. In essence, the performer is called upon to play, or perform, the multiple roles related to his or her own life and own identity. This concept is closely related to communication theory's concepts of identity and roles. However, it differs slightly in terms of focus. While communication theory is interested in how we play our social roles in conjunction with others, performance is more interested in how we create and frame our behavior as part of a performative "act." For example, Julie is a student as well as a waitress. Each of these roles requires a different performance. Likewise, the setting and the audience is different for each performance. Julie must adapt to these differences in order for her performance to be successful. When she is playing the role of a student, she may be wearing jeans and a T-shirt. She must sit at a desk inside a classroom and listen to her professor lecture on the material. If she has a question, Julie knows she must raise her hand to get the professor's attention. Her role of a student also requires her to write papers and take exams. When Julie is playing the role of a waitress, she must wear the uniform required by the restaurant in which she works. She also has a different set of actions to perform. She must introduce herself to the customers, take their orders, and deliver the food to their tables. She also has a particular dialogue in which she must engage, such as asking the customers if they would like coffee or dessert after they have finished their meal, or asking if they are ready for the check. Julie knows that each of her roles takes place within a specific performance environment and, for the most part, is maintained within that environment. In other words, Julie would not raise her hand in order to ask one of her customers if they would like some coffee, nor would she begin each class session by saying, "Hi, my name is Julie and I will be taking care of you this morning."

On a practical level, the performance of everyday life enables us to develop an individual identity as well as create and maintain a social identity. The roles we perform as agents in the performance of everyday life are heightened and framed in some way. They are affected by the settings we find ourselves in as well as the audience with whom we must interact. Ethically, we must perform each of our roles according to social norms or societal expectations. If the norms are not followed, or the expectations are violated in some way, the role becomes ineffective or at least called into question. For example, if Julie showed up to class barefoot and wearing a bikini, her performance in the role of student would be questioned by those around her. Furthermore, if she refused to wait on customers at the restaurant, or took their order while shouting at them and calling them names, she would be fired from her role as waitress.

Literary Performance

In traditional literary performance, the performer is often referred to as a *narrator* or *character*. Oftentimes the term *speaker* is used as a general reference to the speaker of the text. Narrators and characters are created by the author of the text in order to tell the story. Stories may contain a first-person "I" narrator who tells his or her own story to the listener, or a third-person narrator who tells the story of the other characters while using "he" and "she" pronouns. The performer, in turn, embodies the role of the narrator and/or the characters in order to bring the story to life for an audience.

In order to gain a deeper understanding of the narrator, character, or speaker who will be performed, it is often helpful for the performer to ask a series of questions concerning the characterization or traits of the narrator/character/speaker. The first question the performer might ask is, "*Who* is speaking?" The "who" can be analyzed *physically* (appearance of face and body, clothing, health, etc.), *emotionally* (mood, personality, attitudes, outlook on life), *socially* (occupation, economic status, relationships with others, group affiliations), and *morally* (values, ethical sense of right and wrong, degree of trustworthiness). The second question is, "*What* is the subject or topic being discussed?" Perhaps the narrator or character is remembering an event from the past, complaining about his or her job, or gossiping about another individual. The third question is, "*To whom* does the speaker speak?" Does he or she speak to him or herself? A group of strangers? A therapist? A deceased relative? A generalize audience? The fourth question is "*When* and *where* does the telling take place?" In other words, what is the scene or setting? The story may specify a particular location along with a particular time, day, season, or year. For example, in the Robert Frost poem, *Stopping By Woods on a Snowy Evening*, the text specifies that it is evening, it is snowing, and the location is beside the woods. The fifth question is, "*How* does the speaker speak?" Does the character have a particular accent? Does the narrator speak in rhyme or use metaphors? Does he or she ramble? Are there long stretches of silence? Is there a chronological telling of events? The final question is, "*Why* does the speaker of the text speak?" What is the purpose behind the telling of the story? Does the narrator or character speak to unburden him or herself? To come to grips with his or her grief? To apologize? To scold? To explain his or her actions? In answering these questions about the speaker and the story being told, the performer is faced with varying degrees of sureness. Hopkins and Long explain that the answers the performer seeks can take the form of *certainties* (givens or known facts specified within the text), *probabilities* (very likely, although not stated outright), or *possibilities* (based only on the slightest of hints, inferred from the language or activities within the text). The more characteristics the performer is able to glean about the speaker of the text, the more fully developed the performance of that narrator or character will be. For example, in the poem "Her Story" by Naomi Long Madgett, the speaker says, "They named me Grace and waited for a light and agile dancer." She then explains that instead, "I turned out big and black and burly." Grace goes on to state that she always wanted to be an actress on Broadway and play the role of Juliet. Unfortunately she didn't look the part, so she ended up being a waitress in Harlem. By reading this poem, the performer knows for certain that the speaker is a female named Grace, she is big and black and burly, and she is a waitress in Harlem. These facts are stated outright in the text. It is probable that Grace is unhappy. She doesn't state this directly, but it is very likely based on the fact that she had to give up her dream. It is also probable that she tried to commit suicide because she reveals, "I tried the wrong solution. The stuff I drank made me deathly sick and someone called a doctor." There are no certainties or probabilities as to whom Grace speaks. However, based on her language and activities, it is possible that she is speaking to a psychiatrist. It is also possible that she is speaking to one of her customers inside the Harlem restaurant. In this case, it would be left up to the performer to decide to whom the speaker speaks.

In the performance of poems, short stories, and novels, the agent functions to bring the narrator, characters, and story to life for the audience. The performer has reached his or her own understanding of the literary text and desires to share that understanding with the audience. The ethical implications of performing literary texts rests in being true to the author's intent. Though many literary texts are open to various interpretations, the performer must be careful not to distort the text. A *distortion* occurs when a performer ignores a given certainty, opting instead to perform the text according to his or her own liking. In other words, a performer should not play Grace as a perky blonde model. To do so would be a distortion of the poem.

Nontraditional or Alternative Performance

Nontraditional or alternative performance styles include personal narratives, ethnographic performance, and avant-garde performance. In a *personal narrative*, the performer tells a story from his or her own life. The narrative may recount an embarrassing moment, a humorous event, an act of bravery, a personal triumph, and so on. When telling the story to an audience, the performer takes on the role of *storyteller*. The performer, then, becomes a "character" in the story being told. In other words, the "I" in the story becomes a separate entity from the "I" performer who is telling the story. For example, Amanda may want to share the story about the time she donated her hair to Locks of Love. In her narrative, she may recount the months that it took to grow her hair to the required length, the apprehension about her decision which she shared with her friend, the interaction that took place with the beautician who cut her hair, the feelings of sadness that she experienced after having lost her long hair, and the sense of joy she felt knowing that her hair would benefit a child in need. During the performance of her narrative, Amanda might give different voices and mannerisms to the characters of her friend and the beautician, but she would also use a different tone of voice and different mannerisms to distinguish the character of herself as participant in the action, and herself as storyteller.

Again, personal narratives are a heightened form of storytelling in which the story is aesthetically framed for an audience. We are all, by nature, storytellers, and personal narratives allow us to share our life experiences with others. Further, personal narratives allow the performer to reveal his or her personal values with an audience. Additionally, the expression of this value system enables the performer to form a common bond with the audience who may identify with the cultural values expressed by the performer. For this reason, the performer of the personal narrative has an ethical obligation to tell the story as accurately as possible. If an audience learns that the events and experiences have been fabricated, the performer's ethos will be damaged and his or her integrity called into question.

In ethnographic performance, the performer does not "perform" himself or herself, but instead must perform the role of the *other*. In order to construct an ethnographic performance, the performer must observe and/or interview a particular group of individuals, usually collecting a set of narratives from the group. After interviewing and/or observing a particular group and collecting the narratives, the ethnographic performer scripts the interviews or narratives into a performance and performs the stories for an audience. For example, for her performance of *Fires in the Mirror*, Anna Deveare Smith interviewed members of both the black and Jewish communities in the Crown Heights area of Brooklyn, New York, to find out how they felt about the rioting and hatred expressed between the two communities after a Jewish man ran over an African American youth who was riding a bicycle. Smith embodied these various individuals as she recounted their experiences and feelings within her performance. Likewise, for *The Exonerated*, Jessica Blank and Eric Jensen traveled across the United States and interviewed individuals who had served anywhere from two to twenty-two years on death row and who were later found innocent and released by the state. They wanted to know what it was like not only to be convicted of a crime that you did not commit, but to be sentenced to death for that crime. Unlike Smith, Blank and Jensen did not embody these exonerated individuals themselves, but instead created a script which enabled other performers to take on the roles of these freed former inmates.

Practically speaking, ethnographic performance allows the performer to both develop an understanding of a particular group of individuals and to share that understanding with an audience.

However, because the content of ethnographic performance centers around actual living human beings, the ethnographic performer is bound by particularly strong ethical obligations. Because the performer must embody the individuals whose stories are being told, special care must be taken by the performer to present the *others* as accurately as possible, not only in the content of their stories, but in voice, emotions, mannerisms, and possibly, even appearance.

In avant-garde performance, the performer becomes an instrument of social change. The avant-garde performer, also called a *performance artist*, uses performance to directly reflect his or her personal or social concerns. The performance artists may draw upon a variety of mediums such as poetry, dance, music, painting, video, and his or her own body to construct a performance which merges art and life. The content of the performance usually revolves around, to some degree, the performer's personal attitude or value system. Rarely is the performer a character as in a traditional performance, nor does the performance follow a traditional plot line. Instead, the performance becomes, or takes on the characteristics of, a work of art. The performer is the artist and the artist is the performer. For example, performance artist Karen Finley relies upon the method of avant-garde performance to help her work through her emotional rage and pain over her father's death. In one particular performance, Finley expresses her outrage over the fact that the mourners at her father's funeral seemed more interested in eating the food than in paying their respects to the deceased. To visualize this rage, Finley, at one point in the performance, drops her pants and proceeds to smear canned yams over her bare buttocks. She follows this up with a string of foul-mouthed obscenities.

Generally speaking, avant-garde performers use performance as a means of discovering or exploring some personal or social truth and bringing that truth to light for an audience. The performer, as the agent of change, challenges the audience, through the performance, to become critically involved and reexamine or reevaluate its own social, political, or cultural value system. The performance artist works under very few ethical constraints. Though it is unlikely the performance artist would intentionally bring physical harm or injury to the audience, he or she may, in fact, inflict bodily harm on him or herself to elicit an emotional response. The infliction of bodily harm, however, is reserved for professional avant-garde performers and should not be used in classroom performances.

Agent Exercises

Perception Exercise #1: Communication Theory

1. You have been struggling with writing your paper for your communication class. Your professor seems truly interested in helping students do their best work, so you decide to go to her office to discuss your paper. As you approach your professor's office, you hear two voices and they seem to be arguing. Another student from your class comes out of your professor's office, muttering under his breath, "What a b——!"

   a. What do you do next? Do you go into the professor's office or decide to come back another time?

   b. What led you to make the decision that you made?

   c. List the stimuli that were involved in leading you to make that decision.

Perception Exercise #2: Communication Theory

2. Over the next week, pick one social setting (a party, meeting, class, meal, etc.). Observe what happens during this event. Then interview 3 people who also attended this event and ask them what they thought about the event. For example, what stood out to them? How would they describe this event to someone who wasn't there? What did they find interesting or boring? Compare their responses.

a. What similarities were there in their responses to the event? Why do you think they saw the event in similar ways?

b. What differences were there in their responses to the event? Why do you think they saw the event in different ways?

Role Exercise #1: Communication Theory

1. As you go about your day tomorrow, list all the roles that you fulfill. Of all these roles, which ones are the most important to you? Do you think the roles that are most important to you now are likely to change in the future? Why or why not?

Role Exercise #2: Communication Theory

2. Pick one of the roles from your list in Exercise 1. What expectations do you have for that role? Analyze how well you think you performed your role that day.

Self Exercise #1: Communication Theory

1. If you have a MySpace or Facebook page, how do you describe yourself on that page? If you don't have such a page, how would you describe yourself on such a page? Use any description that represents your personality, character and appearance.

   a. Did you develop an accurate or creative description of yourself? Would your friends think it's accurate?

   b. What other attributes might you include on such a page?

   c. Which of these descriptions are elements of your self that is more public and which are elements of your self that is more private? As you place these descriptors on a continuum think about whether you have limits on who has access to this information about you and how you would feel if someone to whom you have not given permission to access your page read these things about you.

Self Exercise #2: Communication Theory

2. List one aspect of yourself that you really like. How did you develop this attribute? That is, were you born with it? Did an experience in your life lead you to develop this attribute? Did someone who is important to you influence you in its development? List one aspect of yourself that you don't like. How might you go about changing this attribute?

Ethos Exercise #1: Rhetoric

1. As a class, come up with an elected position that each student will "run" for. Drawing from your actual experience, create a short speech that shows that you possess the ethos that makes you right for the job.

Ethos Exercise #2: Rhetoric

2. Find a recruiting poster or pamphlet produced by another university. Analyze the ways that the institution demonstrates its ethos through reference to its policies, history, and organizational structure.

Persona Exercise #1: Rhetoric

1. Recall a time in your past when you tried, and "failed," to create a persona in conversation with others to achieve some goal (even if that goal was strictly relational, as in trying to impress some girl/boy). Focus specifically on the verbal strategies you used to create this persona.

Persona Exercise #2: Rhetoric

2. Do the same analysis above for someone in the public eye, whether a politician or some figure in popular culture, like an actor or entertainer.

Interest Exercise #1: Rhetoric

1. Define a strictly personal interest that you have which expresses itself in some habit. Explain under what conditions this interest may (or already has) become a rhetorical interest that requires you to engage other people to address some issue.

Interest Exercise #2: Rhetoric

2. Find a *New York Times* (online at nytimes.com) and read over the letters to the editor on the editorial page that are collected under a single theme. What common interests do you see expressed? What interests are different? What interests may possibly be hidden?

Constraint Exercise #1: Rhetoric

1. Think of a time as a child when you had a "big idea" and tried to get others to work with you to get something done. Define the situation and the internal and external constraints that you had to overcome to be successful or which prevented that success.

Constraint Exercise #2: Rhetoric

2. Read the editorial page of the a newspaper or magazine and find a full-length editorial that describes or reveals some public problem. Underline passages that identify some constraints to addressing this problem and then interpret these passages in rhetorical terms.

Everyday Life Exercise #1: Performance

1. Make a list of the roles you play in your everyday life. Choose one specific role from this list and explain how you change your actions, language, and appearance in order to play or perform this role.

Everyday Life Exercise #2: Performance

2. Create a personal CD which will serve to introduce you to the class. Your CD should be a visual and auditory presentation of your many roles and identities. Create a cover for your CD as well as a list of 6–8 songs which help describe you as an individual.

Literary Exercise #1: Performance

1. You will be placed in groups of 3–4 individuals. Each group will be given the printed lyrics from one of the songs used in the everyday life Exercise #2. Analyze the levels of characterization of the speaker of this text. First, analyze the speaker physically, emotionally, socially, and morally. Second, analyze the dramatic situation occurring in this text: What does the speaker speak about? To whom does the speaker speak? Where and when does the speaker speak? Why does the speaker speak? Indicate whether your answers to these questions are based on certainties, probabilities, or possibilities.

Literary Exercise #2: Performance

2. Select one of the following poems: "An Apology for Wolves" by Peter Wild or "The Serpent" by Theodore Roethke. Create or describe two different speakers and two different scenes that could be used by a performer to perform this poem. Be sure to support your choices with specific clues or indicators from the text that aided in your decision.

Nontraditional Exercise #1: Performance

1. Personal narratives may range from humorous to serious in tone and may revolve around any personal life experience. However, inherent in all personal narratives is a moral or lesson to be learned which, in turn, helps to strengthen our identity and sense of self-worth. The moral or lesson also allows us to make a connection with the audience by reinforcing a common social value. For this exercise, tell the story of your greatest lesson ever learned. What social value or values are upheld in your story?

Nontraditional Exercise #2: Performance

2. Choose two different outside groups to observe. The groups could include your church congregation, patients waiting in a doctor's office, or even prospective adoptees at a PetSmart adoption day. Contrast these two groups by answering the following questions: A) What is the purpose of the gathering? B) What is the overall emotional tone of the gathering? C) Who are the participants (sex, age, social status, or an other relevant category)? D) What are the rules of interaction? In other words, how does the setting or environment affect the behavior of these groups?

Nontraditional Exercise #3: Performance

3. As we will learn later, one feature of avant-garde performance is the element of incongruity. When a performer incorporates incongruity into an avant-garde piece, he or she combines a series of seemingly unrelated actions, words, phrases, or sentences in order to create a performance. For this activity, you will be placed in groups of 4–6 individuals. Choose one specific phrase or action from Exercise #1 in the Performance of Everyday Life section. You will be given 10 minutes to prepare a performance which incorporates each single physical action or verbal statement from each person in the group.

Section 2

Audience

The audience in communication refers generally to those with whom the agent communicates.

The Audience in Communication Theory

For communication theorists, the audience is not someone *out there*, but is someone with whom the speaker (agent) has a relationship for which both parties are responsible. We adapt to our audience based on the situation, our relationship with the others involved, and our knowledge of those others. Because communication theorists view the agent and the audience as being in relationship with each other, both have responsibility for the interaction. We select our behaviors and react to others' behaviors based on our expectations related to the situation and whether our expectations are being met. The nature of the relationship, however, helps to define the situation and therefore what is considered to be effective and appropriate communication in the setting. The audience then might be a friend or family member; a boss, employee, or coworker; a stranger on a plane or train; or some unknown group of people who are likely to read your blog or see your video on YouTube. In all these situations, the agent wants to present certain elements of his or her self to others. How we present ourselves to these others depends to some extent on what we hope they will take from what we have to say. With this in mind, communication theorists tend to think of the ***audience*** as a particular other or group of others with whom we are in relationship.

Other(s)

A key developmental milestone in childhood is the realization that we are individuals apart from those around us. Once we begin to develop a sense of self as a separate entity, we also begin to develop a sense of others as separate entities and being in relation with them. The ***other*** is the recipient of our messages. We adapt our behavior in order to have the other, hopefully, interpret our message in the way that we desire. The other may be someone that we know well, such as a friend or close family member, or may be unknown to us, such as someone reading our blog. When we know someone well, it is easier for us to predict how he or she will interpret our messages, although misunderstandings can still occur.

As we discussed in the section on the agent, we desire to have others think of us in certain ways. Communication theorists are particularly interested in how we adapt our behavior for different audiences in order to accomplish our goals. For example, if you need a favor, such as borrowing a car, do you ask your best friend or one of your parents in the same way or do you frame your request based on your knowledge of that person and your history together? Would you ask your boss or an acquaintance if you could borrow his or her car? In all of these situations, you not only want to accomplish the goal of borrowing the car, but you also want to present yourself to the other person as responsible so that he or she will trust you with it.

Groups and Social Norms

For this class, when we talk about groups, we are not talking so much about task groups, such as the ones that we join in a college classroom for an assignment. The groups of interest here are *social groups* that share a common set of values and expectations about what behaviors are expected, obligated, or forbidden, including what we should say and how we should say it.

Across the course of our lives, we will become members of a wide range of groups. Look back at the introductory section on the history of communication theory when we discussed how you came to develop your sense of self through your interaction with others (remember Symbolic Interaction). As children, we are born into certain social groups based on nationality, ethnicity, socioeconomic status, sex, religion, etc. These group memberships are defined for us by our biology or our parents' choices. As we get older, we choose additional groups to join, such as professions, shared interest groups, political parties, etc. *Socialization* is the process through which we learn to be a member of a social group. Primary socialization teaches us our culture (the language, values and beliefs of our primary group—family, ethnic, social class, nationality) and secondary socialization teaches us how to be a member of groups after early childhood. The socialization process teaches us how to behave in ways that lets others know that we are members of a certain group. We desire to show to other members of the group that we belong. As such, members of the group become our audience so that we can demonstrate our belonging.

Social groups develop rules for behavior. When we want others to know that we know these rules and demonstrate our ability to act in the prescribed ways, we are revealing our membership in the group. The group members become our audience as we demonstrate our membership in the group. For example, in college we begin to develop our professional identity and want to reveal to campus recruiters that we have the knowledge, skills, and abilities to become a member of a profession by being hired by this organization. We think carefully about what clothes to wear to the interview, what activities we want to highlight, and how to answer questions. The selections we make are based on our assessment of the interviewer as a particular audience member in a particular situation.

Social and Personal Relationships

Social relationships are those relationships we have with others that are based on our public selves. We do not need to know the deep, dark secrets of our coworkers, group members on class projects, service providers, etc. However, life goes more smoothly when we have pleasant exchanges with others, whether accomplishing a task for work or getting checked out in a store. We can act in fairly scripted ways to accomplish our goals and demonstrate our competence in a wide range of social settings. In these cases, the audience members are the others who are involved in the event. Everyone needs to follow the script for the event to go smoothly. What happens when you are in a store and cannot get someone who works there to answer your questions or help you with a heavy object? How do you adapt your behavior to get good service?

Personal relationships are those relationships with others with whom we share more of our private selves. We know considerable amounts of personal information (e.g., attitudes, preferences, experiences) about other family members and they know a lot about us. When we are developing friendships, the most predictable way to become friends is to share information about ourselves and find out what we have in common. *Self-disclosure* is the process through which we share more and more of our private selves with others. Just by looking at you, someone else probably wouldn't know how you feel about sushi or gay rights. While you may not care if others know how you feel about these issues, you might care if they know how you feel about some things. In personal relationships, because we know so much about each other through lots of self-disclosure, we can adapt our behavior in ways that are most meaningful to the other person. Buying a gift that is "just right" for a close friend or family member can be easy because we know so much about what they like.

When we are interacting with others then, we think about the nature of our relationship and adapt our behavior to fit the expectations we have of each other. The "right" thing to say or do in a situation depends on our relationship with the other person. If you and a coworker have a strictly social (in this case, professional) relationship, then it would not be appropriate to talk about the wild party that you attended over the weekend. If you and this coworker talk about shared concerns, such as balancing the demands of the job with the demands of having a toddler, then you are moving from a strictly social relationship to a more personal one. If you and this coworker went to that wild party together, then you probably think of each other more as friends than as coworkers.

Situational Constraints

What is considered appropriate and effective communication depends on the situation. The ***situation*** includes the social and physical environment. The *social environment* consists of not only the individuals that are present, but also the roles that they are playing. Some examples of social environments include a party, a family gathering, going to the movies with friends, working on a class project in a group, and attending a rally on campus.

The *physical environment* includes the setting or place of the interaction. If you visit a friend at work, you are likely to interact with him or her in a way that you think is appropriate for his or her place of work instead of the way that you interact when hanging out at home.

Part of adapting to our audience is "reading" the situation and adapting our behavior appropriately. This adaptation is a complex process of reading all the elements of the situation because what appears to be the same situation may have a range of expectations. For example, weddings are highly ritualized events and yet we act differently if a wedding is set in a church or a garden. While the wedding is the social environment, the church and the garden reflect the physical environment. We will adapt our behavior in myriad ways in order to be seen as playing our role of "wedding guest" appropriately. Our definition of what is appropriate behavior may change, however, when we shift from the wedding ceremony to the reception. The social and physical environments of these events are both different, but are also related to an overarching script for wedding day events. A person who sat quietly in the church during the ceremony may dance and drink at the reception. While dancing and drinking during the reception may be quite acceptable, it is probably less acceptable behavior during the ceremony.

The Audience in Rhetoric

The *audience* of rhetorical discourse is the complement of the agent. Where the rhetor is a conscious instigator of social action, a rhetorical audience is the group of people who are instigated. They are that group of people able to be persuaded by rhetoric and capable of acting in such a way as to effect social change. One way of understanding a rhetorical audience is to see it as a both a target and a tool. One *targets* that audience which is able to act as a *tool* for some productive end. In advertising, this notion of audience is employed for very narrow ends of getting specific demographic groups interested in purchasing a product. In rhetoric, the productive ends are associated with more general questions of social policy or moral values.

Audience

We often think of the audience for rhetoric as the sum of all of the people who "hear" a speech. In ancient times, this would be the citizens gathered in the public square; in modern times, this would be the people who experience a speech through all the mediums of mass communication. This is the *empirical* audience, or the audience that physically exists in a particular place and time and hears a speech when it is given. The empirical audience is useful to know when trying to predict the actual effects one's rhetoric will have on an audience. The power of political advertising is often determined by the number and type of person exposed to its message.

However, the empirical audience is not the most useful concept to use when creating or interpreting rhetorical discourse. When creating rhetoric, the most useful concept is that of the target audience. A *target audience* is that group of people both able to be persuaded and capable of acting in such a way to facilitate the interests of the rhetor. Identifying a target audience beforehand is crucial to sculpting a message that actually produces social consequences because it allows a rhetor to overcome internal constraints of the people in the best position to initiate change. For example, political analysts often discuss how certain politicians target married women or NASCAR dads or senior citizens because they are most able to cast votes favorable to a particular candidate. While we might see this as a cynical appeal to a narrow selection of voters, it is a common truth that someone trying to be all things to all people ends up being nothing to no one. If a politician wasted time trying to persuade an audience either incapable of producing effective consequences (like those below voting age) or unwilling to be persuaded due to internal constraints (like those who strictly adhere to the ideology of a different political party) then their rhetoric would evaporate into the empty air.

The identification of a target audience is typically only half the process, however. A rhetor must then construct a common "identity" that is recognizable and appealing to the target audience. The *evoked audience* is this textual construction of the audience created by the rhetor for the purposes of persuasion. Like the concept of *persona*, the evoked audience is a literary or hypothetical identity that exists separately from the actual diversity and character of the people listening to a speech. In this sense, the evoked audience is a kind of "second" persona, another "fiction." The function of the evoked audience is to create an attractive image of unity that makes members of an audience desire to be a part of it by acting collectively toward the same end. In its most general form, we find politicians using evoked audiences whenever they speak of the "American people" as a collective body of people who love liberty, freedom, and democracy. By creating a category of identity that can unify a group of separate individuals, an evoked audience creates the possibility of cooperative action.

Today, we often think of the term "American people" as the expression of a political platitude, but during the founding of the country it had a very productive application. In contrast to those who thought themselves either subjects of Britain or members of separate states, the term "American" made possible a national identity that both brought together the colonies and separated them from the British monarchy. These two actions will be further elaborated in Identification and Polarization.

As with *persona*, one must be careful not to assume that the target and the evoked audiences are the same. Like persona, the evoked audience often is what a rhetor wants an audience to be rather than what they are. A collection of teenagers may all be good at a certain sport but they are not yet a "team" until the coach starts telling them that they are. The coach's rhetoric thus creates a sense of commonality by "evoking" the team spirit within the individual players that may not have been present before. Or even more cynically, sometimes the evoked audience is used to exploit the desires of the target audience without ever expecting or even desiring them to achieve this ideal. This strategy is ubiquitous in advertising, where the common strategy is to first target a specific demographic population and then imply that by purchasing a product one becomes a new and better person even when that is clearly unlikely. For example, ads tell us that we will become sexier by buying a new car or more powerful by wearing an expensive suit, thus creating a fictional persona to which we aspire and then providing us a convenient means to achieve that persona—purchasing the product. That we will never actually become that person is not the concern for advertisers so long as we spend our money. They target the audience that they believe will strive after the persona that they evoke and invest money to become that type of person. The evoked audience can thus be used to persuade an audience to behave in such a way that benefits mostly the author of the message and not the hearers.

Identification

When we "identify" with someone we see ourselves as sharing some quality or experience with another person or group. Usually this feeling comes after the revelation of a life experience that we see as similar to our own, even if that experience occurred within a wholly different social context. The process of making friends with people often begins with this process of identification where two strangers find themselves sharing in some common interest, habit, belief, or feeling. Two children may both like the same cartoon or two neighbors may share similar political beliefs. This process of establishing a relationship also functions in fictional contexts. When we read a book or go to the movies, our enjoyment typically depends on how well we "identify" with the main character. In this sense, the process of identification is how two or more people come to form a bond that generates commonality through shared interests.

In rhetoric, *identification* describes the process by which a rhetor draws parallels and makes connections between his or her *persona* and the *evoked audience* in an effort to establish an *actual* connection with the *target audience*. In other words, it represents the persuasive attempt on the part of the rhetorical agent to say "I am one of you" in order to create a sense of "we." The justification for such a strategy is that we tend to prefer listening to people who speak and think like ourselves. Especially in politics, we want our leaders to reaffirm our values, legitimate our goals, and speak from our common history. Consequently, as much as we often hear people claim that we just want politicians who "tell the truth," we really want politicians who tell the truths we want to hear. The same goes for people we generally think of as friends. Opposites may attract at first, but only people who share very basic attitudes and values tend to stay together.

Distinction

Identification, however, is not always the most effective rhetorical strategy. Especially in times of uncertainty when we seek out not loyal friendship but good advice, we often look to those people who are very *unlike* us in that they possess expertise in a very specific subject. In this case we look not for identification but *distinction*, or the characteristic of being separate and often superior to the group to which an audience belongs. Thus, when "experts" seek to influence policy decisions, their rhetorical strategy is usually to set themselves apart from others and by doing so establish their authority as possessors of special knowledge. Whether those experts are scientists, theologians, ethicists, economists, or movie critics, they all base their arguments on the principles derived from a specialized discourse not accessible to the general public.

In cases of *distinction*, then, the persona of the rhetor stands *apart* from the evoked audience. In cases of *identification*, the persona of the rhetor is *fused* with that of the evoked audience. Both represent forms of credibility, but distinction is credibility from expertise while identification is credibility from likeness. Determining whether an audience will respond to a rhetor who stands *apart from* them or stands *with* them may be the most important factor to know for any rhetor who seeks to influence their decisions.

Polarization

Like the positive and negative sides of a magnetic field, a "polarity" represents one end of a divided spectrum to which things are attracted or repelled. Thus, when a metallic object is placed within that magnetic spectrum it must go either one way or the other; there is no "in-between." Society often behaves in much the same manner. As individuals we often are forced to choose between aligning ourselves with one group or another with little room for compromise. In high school we must choose between cliques; in college we must choose between majors; in professional life we must choose careers; in politics we must choose political parties; in religion we must choose faiths. In all these situations there is, of course, the decision not to choose, but this choice, too, has consequences, for then you risk being abandoned or ignored.

By its nature as an art that thrives in conflict and uncertainty, rhetorical discourse often magnifies these choices and uses the contrast to force us into a decision. *Polarization* is the rhetorical strategy of contrasting the norms and choices of a *criticized audience* unfavorably with those of the *evoked audience* in order to encourage people to be like "us" rather than like "them." This *criticized audience* typically represents either the group in competition with the rhetor's interests, like another political party, or simply a demonized audience that is used as a convenient foil, like a group of "traitors" or "evil-doers." The strategy is then to argue that if one does not follow the path preferred by the rhetor and his or her evoked audience, then they will align themselves with a group of people who lack ethical or practical judgment. Most children become acquainted with this strategy early on in their lives when they are encouraged to behave during the year so that Santa Claus includes them on his "nice" rather than his "naughty" list. This same model can be applied effectively in the analysis of contemporary partisan politics.

The process of audience analysis must therefore include not just the nature of one's target audience, but also what groups that target audience sees themselves as being competitive with, different from, and superior to. A rhetor can then choose from these groups the one that can most effectively be used within a polarization strategy as a criticized audience.

The Audience in Performance

Audience in performance refers to the group of individuals who have assembled to view or take part in the performance. The audience, like the performer or agent, can play a variety of roles in the area of performance. These roles are usually distinguished by the degree of participation audience members have within the performance. Audiences may remain completely passive, simply viewing the performance as it takes place, or they may become quite active by actually taking part in the creation of the performance. Regardless of the degree of participation, however, the audience is a necessary component for performance. To borrow the adage, if a tree falls in the forest and no one is there to hear it, does it really make a sound? Without the audience, the impact of the performance would suffer greatly.

Performer's Audience *v.* Speaker's Audience

Quite simply, the *performer's audience* consists of those individuals who are watching the performance. This audience is similar to rhetoric's empirical audience. The *speaker's audience* is the person or persons to whom the speaker, narrator, or character speaks. While all types of performances contain a performer's audience, usually only literary performances will contain a speaker's audience.

The relationship between the speaker and the speaker's audience is described as open or closed depending upon whether the speaker's audience exists inside or outside of the performance text. In a *closed* performance, the speaker addresses his or her audience (or listener) within the world of the text. The performance takes place behind the theatrical "fourth wall" as the performer's audience becomes observers or eavesdroppers of the performance. Closed performances are common in traditional dramatic plays as well as in most television shows and movies. In closed performances, the audience remains quite passive. In an *open* performance, the fourth wall is removed and the speaker speaks directly to the performer's audience. A performer may opt for an open performance in order to allow the performer's audience to substitute for or play the role of the speaker's audience. For example, in the short story *My Sister's Marriage* by Cynthia Rich, the speaker, Sarah Ann, addresses a group of listeners whom she refers to as "strangers" or "outsiders." In an open performance of this short story, the performer playing the role of Sarah Ann may chose to cast her audience in the role of these strangers or outsiders, addressing them directly, and thus, breaking the imaginary fourth wall. The performer's audience then is drawn into and becomes part of the performance instead of simply "eavesdropping" on the action. Many times a performer will choose to present a work via an open performance because it serves to heighten the emotional involvement of the audience. Since the audience is spoken to on personal level, the performance becomes more immediate. The audience can no longer simply sit back and observe from the sidelines.

Additionally, a performance may alternate between an open and closed performance. A Chamber Theatre production, for instance, contains a narrator who speaks directly to the performer's audience, telling them a story. At the same time, the performance contains characters who speak to each other within the world of the text. The open and closed mixture can also exist in other types of performances. On the television show *Saved By The Bell*, for example, the main character Zack interacts with his classmates Kelly, Jessie, Lisa, Slater, and Screech while the viewing audience looks on. However, there are moments in each episode where Zack breaks the fourth wall by looking at the camera and addressing the viewers at home.

Spectators *v.* Spectactors

The performance audience can also be classified in terms of spectators or spectactors depending upon the degree of involvement in the performance. *Spectators* are passive audience members who simply view the performance. Spectators are most common in aesthetic types of performances such as plays, concerts, movies, or poetry readings. The audience of spectators is set apart from or distanced from the actual performance. They watch the show, but they do not actively participate in the show. On the other hand, *spectactors* are active audience members who participate, in some way or to some degree, in the performance. Spectactors are found in the area of cultural performance. Cultural rituals such as weddings, baby showers, funerals, bar mitzvahs, and even football games require the blending of performance and participation. For example, guests at a baby shower do not simply sit on periphery and gaze at the mother-to-be. They participate by playing games, handing out gifts, eating the prepared food, and conversing with others in attendance. Spectactors, however, are not limited only to cultural performances. They may exist in the realm of aesthetic performance as well. A great example of the spectactor audience in aesthetic performance exists in the play *Tony n' Tina's Wedding*. During this play, the ticket-purchasing audience is called upon to play the role of the wedding and reception guests. Audience members must mingle with the actors in the play, get caught up in disputes between the two families, eat the catered food at the reception, and dance with the other guests on the dance floor.

Accidental Audience *v.* Integral Audience

When discussing performance and ritual, Richard Schechner distinguishes between what he calls the accidental audience and the integral audience. The *accidental audience* is a public audience that voluntarily comes to see the publicaly advertised performance. Generally speaking, aesthetic performances such as plays and movies have accidental audiences. Rituals, on the other hand, contain an *integral audience*. The integral audience is a more privatized group of individuals who come to the performance because they have an obligation to attend or because the event holds a special significance for them. Graduations, baby showers, and communions would contain integral audiences. Again, accidental audiences are more likely to be spectator audiences while integral audiences are almost always composed of spectactors. However, there are exceptions to this norm. Although most plays have accidental audiences, there may be certain VIPs who have received a special invitation to opening night and thereby become integral audience members within the accidental audience. Or, certain individuals may be interested in watching the performance of a ritual in which they take no part. For example, many American viewers may chose to watch the presidential inauguration on television. Yet, they are not participants in the inauguration itself. Therefore, the viewers are accidental audience members who join together with the integral audience members to create the performance.

Audience Exercises

Other Exercise #1: Communication Theory

1. You are having a lot of personal problems and these problems are affecting your performance in your communication class. You haven't talked to the professor or anyone else in class about your problems. As the midterm approaches, you realize that your grade is in trouble in this class and you decide to go talk to the professor. You want this professor to believe that you are serious about improving your grade. What do you know about this professor and how does that knowledge influence how you might approach him or her?

Other Exercise #2: Communication Theory

2. Think about a time when you and a friend have had a disagreement about something that reflected different values (political or religious differences work well for this exercise). Usually in these kinds of disagreements, we spend most of our time and energy on trying to convince the other person that we're right. What would you need to do to try to really understand the other person's point of view? How can you "get inside" his or her head and heart?

Norms Exercise #1: Communication Theory

1. For most people, their families are an important social group. Think of one rule in your family that you feel is particularly unique or important to your family. What is that rule? What expectations are associated with that rule? What happens when someone breaks that rule? Is this rule the same in your friends' families? If not, what is the related rule in another family and what are the expectations associated with it?

Norms Exercise #2: Communication Theory

2. Over the next week, observe one social event (a class, meeting, party, meal, etc.). What are the rules associated with this social event? How are people expected to dress? Who is expected to talk and who is expected to listen? What are they expected to talk about? What subjects are they supposed to avoid? How long are people expected to stay at this event? What happens if people come late or leave early?

Relationships Exercise #1: Communication Theory

1. You are going out to dinner with your boss, a coworker, and a potential client. You and your boss get along well, but haven't spent much time together outside of the office. You and your coworker know each other and have lots of interests in common. The potential client is someone whom you have never met. What topics would be appropriate for conversation during this dinner? What topics would not be appropriate? Why or why not?

Relationships Exercise #2: Communication Theory

2. Think about a classmate whose name you don't know. Do you know his or her favorite kind of music, favorite color, political opinions, religious beliefs, most embarrassing moment, most proud moment, what makes him or her happy or sad? Now think about your best friend. Which of these things do you know about him or her? How did you learn them? How long did you know each other before you knew these things? What role does trust play in sharing the more private types of information you share with your friend? What would happen to your relationship if you shared some of his or her most private information with a stranger?

Constraints Exercise #1: Communication Theory

1. Over the next week, observe at least three different kinds of social events. Focus on such things as who is present, the relationships among the people present, what topics are discussed, how formal or informal the conversation seems. Do these things change according to the kind of social event that you observed? In what ways are they similar and different? How does the physical environment change from one event to the next? In what ways are they similar and different?

Constraints Exercise #2: Communication Theory

2. Develop a script in which two people are being introduced to each other. Write out the dialogue between the introducer and the two people who do not know each other. As you write out the dialogue, consider the social and physical setting. Pick any situation that you like. After writing this dialogue, change at least one aspect of the social or physical setting. Reread the dialogue that you developed. Would you make any changes considering the new situational constraints?

Audience Exercise #1: Rhetoric

1. Bring in a print advertisement for some product that explicitly ties the purchase of the product with the personal qualities of the user. Analyze the probable empirical audience, target audience, and evoked audience, and identify their commonalities and differences.

Audience Exercise #2: Rhetoric

2. Create your own product and briefly sketch out a print advertisement. Then analyze your ad using the three kinds of audiences.

Identification Exercise #1: Rhetoric

1. As a student of a state university, many people who are not university students often want to encourage your support by claiming they "identify" with the student body, whether they are commencements speakers, fundraisers, administrators, performers, or lecturers. Give one example of someone who has done this, interpret their strategies, and describe their possible interests in doing so.

Identification Exercise #2: Rhetoric

2. Imagine that you are getting married to a person who has a famous and very powerful mother or father. As a class, choose a real person who is currently in the "public eye." Now imagine you are having dinner with this person for the first time and are trying to think of things to talk about. Come up with anecdotes from your own life that lead to conversations that you think will establish "identification" with this person.

Distinction Exercise #1: Rhetoric

1. As a class, come up with a controversial topic that deals with a very real and specific problem that students at the university care about and are aware of. Now go out and poll students about whom they would trust to speak intelligently about this topic. Ask them to be as specific as possible, even suggest a specific individual. Return to class and see if you can generalize about what "type" of speaker students feel has distinction.

Distinction Exercise #2: Rhetoric

2. Imagine that all the people in this class are part of a new government that will run the university as a city-state. Invent a position that you believe you are ideally suited for, based on your experience. Then write a short speech that defends your decision based on the strategy of distinction.

Polarization Exercise #1: Rhetoric

1. Children's stories have traditionally been used as ways to instill in young minds codes of right and wrong by comparing the actions of "good" and "bad" characters. Like "The Three Little Pigs," stories are used to teach children what NOT to do and who NOT to be like (so that we not only celebrate the death of the wolf, but look down upon those who build cheap houses). Create a children's fable of your own that uses the strategy of polarization to persuade a young audience to act a certain way by contrasting noble behavior with the behavior of those who act "immorally."

Polarization Exercise #2: Rhetoric

2. Choose one of the speeches provided by your instructor to analyze. Read it through and identify the groups or individuals that the speaker criticizes and uses as the polar opposite of those with whom he or he "identifies." List the specific terms the speaker uses to characterize these groups or individuals and then list the qualities or actions that are associated with them. Finally, explain the rhetorical purpose for pursuing the strategy of polarization.

Audience Exercise #1: Performance

1. You will be divided into groups of 4–6 individuals. From this group, select one speaker and setting from Literary Performance Exercise #2 in the section on Agent. Identify the speaker's audience for this particular selection. Volunteers will be asked to stage a small section of this poem as both an open and closed performance. As an audience member, describe the different emotional impacts you received while playing the role of the performer's audience as opposed to the role of the speaker's audience. If you were one of the performers, describe the difference you felt in performing the poem to the speaker's audience in a closed situation as opposed to the performer's audience in an open situation.

Audience Exercise #2: Performance

2. Select two students from the class to create a performance centering around an everyday activity such as gardening, cooking dinner, getting ready to go out on a date, etc. Those students should be given a few minutes to prepare their performance. During the actual performance, the performers must solicit the help from 1–2 classmates who have, up to this point, been spectators of the performance. These spectators must now become spectactors. Discuss how it felt to be drawn into the performance. How did the participants act or react differently to the performance while being a spectator as opposed to a spectactor?

Audience Exercise #3: Performance

3. Identify a performance event you have recently attended in which you played the role of an accidental audience member. What was the nature of this event? Who were some of the others in attendance? Describe the event and the extent of your participation. Were you a spectator or spectactor? Now identify an event in which you were an integral audience member. What was the nature of this event? Who were some of the others in attendance? Describe the extent of your participation in this event. Were you a spectator or spectactor? Discuss or compare the importance of your presence at each of the two events.

Section 3

Message

The message in communication refers generally to the symbolic acts produced, delivered, or performed by the agent in order to communicate with an audience.

The Message in Communication Theory

Communication theorists view messages as more than the words that we exchange. If we live in communication, then everything we say and do impacts the meanings we construct. ***Messages***, then, reflect action. We communicate to achieve desired goals. Communication theorists examine how we construct messages to achieve our goals. Competent communication requires the selection of appropriate and effective messages that help us achieve our multiple goals—such as presenting a particular image, developing a relationship, and completing a task. Because humans have sophisticated brains that are wired for interaction, we process all these elements rather quickly and smoothly. Communication theorists try to pull all these elements apart to understand how it is that humans manage to communicate so effectively most of the time and how to repair misunderstandings.

Symbols

The messages we exchange are based on symbols. ***Symbols*** are simply things that stand for other things and include words (language) and actions (behaviors) that allow us to convey meaning to others. Groups agree upon the meaning assigned to a symbol. Because symbols are arbitrary devices, the same thing is often referred to by different symbols by different groups. Symbols are also ambiguous so that the same symbol may have many different meanings. We will discuss the nature of this ambiguity further when we talk about meaning and symbols.

Often a goal of communication is to convey a particular meaning to a particular other, so we select the symbols that we use carefully in hopes that people will interpret our messages in the way that we desire. Sounds simple, but it's not! Because social groups assign meaning to symbols, we may have misunderstandings because we have different meanings for the same symbol. Remember when we talked about ***perception*** and how our experiences influence which stimuli receive our attention. Through our experiences, we assign a range of meanings to symbols that are somewhat unique. We then interpret communicative behaviors based on our perceptions and the meanings we assign to those behaviors. If someone else has a different set of meanings, then we are likely to misunderstand each other. Hopefully, as we further discuss symbols by examining language and nonverbal behaviors, how misunderstandings arise will become clearer. We will also discuss this issue further in the section on ***meaning***.

Language

We start learning about symbols at a very early age. Even before we begin to talk, we learn that by pointing, others can identify an object that we desire, such as a bottle or a toy, and they can bring it to us. Through language development, we learn which words represent which things. ***Language*** consists not only of the words that represent things, but also the grammatical structure that tells us how the words relate to each other. Every language has rules about what words mean and how to arrange words into sentences.

We first learn words for concrete objects (e.g., ball, bottle, Mama) and then for more abstract ideas (e.g., love, justice, truth). Around the age of two years, we start to demonstrate understanding of the relationships between words by using two-word sentences (e.g., "dog runs," "Tommy hit," "catch ball"). In this process, we start to identify that some symbols stand for things (nouns) and others stand for action (verbs). As we continue to develop, we are able to convey more complex ideas to others.

We use language to share our thoughts, ideas, and experiences with others and learn about their thoughts, ideas, and experiences. While we may have heard this phrase as children, "Sticks and stones can break my bones, but words will never hurt me," most of us know that words can be powerful. What we say to others matters. We react differently when someone says to us "you're wonderful" as opposed to "you're worthless." When we talked about symbolic interaction, we discussed how we learn about our world through our interactions with others. We not only learn what to call things, but also what meanings are assigned to those things. Thus, through language and communication, we develop our sense of self and share it with others. In the process, we develop our relationships with others and make sense of our lives.

We can use different means for communicating with others through language and behavior (nonverbal communication). *Verbal communication* is spoken language. When we talk to someone else, either face-to-face or over the phone, we are using verbal language. *Written communication* is textual language. When we write someone a letter, email, or text message, we are using written language. While verbal and written language may contain the same content, when we are interacting with others face-to-face, they can read our nonverbal messages as well as our verbal messages, which is the focus of the next section.

Nonverbal Communication

Nonverbal communication includes a wide range of actions or behaviors that accompany spoken words. Nonverbal messages include speech-related elements such as the tone of voice, rate of speech, pitch, etc. and other behaviors such as body language, physical proximity, and dress. When we talk to others face-to-face, we not only can hear what they say and how they say it, but we can see their facial expressions, whether they are making eye contact or not, what gestures they make, and much more. Just as we assign meaning to the words that are spoken, we also assign meaning to these actions. We will discuss the interpretation of nonverbal messages further in the section on ***meaning***. Here, it is important that we think about the messages we send to others through our nonverbal behaviors.

Nonverbal messages serve a number of purposes. They can be used to substitute for language. Sometimes a hug conveys more meaning than anything we can say when trying to comfort a friend who is distressed. They can be used to emphasize a verbal message, such as when we pound our fist on the table when trying to make a point. They can contradict a verbal message, such as when we say "nothing's wrong" while avoiding eye contact and shrugging. They can be used to show who we are through the clothes we choose to wear. They can be used to show how we feel about someone. For example, we may show our concern and interest by paying attention (making eye contact, leaning forward, nodding as we listen) when someone else speaks. They can regulate interaction, such as knowing when you can step into a conversation. They can provide feedback so that we know if the other person understands the point we are making.

The Message in Rhetoric

The *message* of rhetorical discourse is the product of intentional persuasion. That is to say, while we often engage in subtle forms of indirect or even unconscious persuasion in our everyday life, rhetoric stands apart as an act of communication that employs persuasive strategies in order to achieve a specific purpose. Being able to understand, implement, and recognize such persuasive components of rhetoric allows us to more effectively act in public settings and make better judgments of the rhetoric of others.

Reasoning

Reasoning, in its most general sense, is the use of reasons to defend or arrive at a conclusion. Whenever we debate with ourselves or with others about why one thing or action is better than another, we engage in the process of reasoning. Thus, a statement of fact or belief on its own, such as "It will rain today," only becomes an expression of reasoning when it is defended or justified, such as with the observation that "There are dark clouds on the horizon." By incorporating reasons for our beliefs, we make our thought process more complex and capable of modification.

In rhetorical discourse, reasoning is tied to the process of argument. As a form of argument, rhetoric relies heavily on the use of reasoning to persuade others of the "reasonableness" of a position by "making a case" for it through the employment of principles, logic, and evidence. These connections between argument, reason, language, and thought were so close in classical Greece that they used the same word, *logos*, as a name for all four concepts. *Logos* referred to all the ways that arguments used the language of reason to stimulate and direct thought.

There are four major forms of reasoning:

1. *Deductive Reasoning.* A "deduction" is a specific conclusion that follows from a more general principle. We reason deductively whenever we start with a universal "truth" and try to apply it to a particular situation to assist in prediction, definition, or control. In it simplest form, it is to take a general principle like "All humans are mortal" and use it to conclude that I, too, will someday die because I am human. Or it is to stay home on Sunday morning in the assumption that "All stores open late on Sunday." In rhetoric, rhetors use deductive reasoning whenever they argue for a specific position on the basis of a universally accepted truth. Women's rights are justified because "all men and women are created equal," a war is authorized because of "all states have a right to self-defense," or the death

penalty is condemned because the Bible says "Thou shalt not kill." The strength of deductive reasoning hinges on how deeply an audience shares the principles from which the rhetor draws his or her conclusions.

2. *Inductive Reasoning.* An "induction" is the opposite of a "deduction." Rather than moving from the general to the particular, it moves from the particular to the general. The process of induction takes a specific observation or experience, like the first taste of a sour lemon, and draws from it a general conclusion that "all lemons are sour." It is also known as argument by specific example. In rhetoric, rhetors use inductive reasoning whenever they point to repeated instances of a thing or event as an indicator of a more general condition. For example, the repeated loss of jobs is used to prove an economic recession, the repeated rejection of minority applicants is used to justify accusations of racism, or the repeated mistakes of a politician are used to prove general incompetence. The legitimacy of inductive reasoning often rests on the capacity for the rhetor to prove that these examples are not isolated cases but are numerous and consistent enough to represent a pattern.

3. *Causal Reasoning.* We see causal reasoning wherever we are encouraged to act (or not act), based upon a cause-and-effect analysis. They are embodied in "if-then" statements of the kind "Put on your coat, because if you go outside without a jacket, then you will get cold." In rhetoric, rhetors use causal reasoning whenever they argue for actions because of the pragmatic consequences. To debate whether lowering the drinking age will increase alcohol abuse among minors, whether enforcing environmental regulations will inhibit economic growth, or whether aggressive antiterrorism legislation will limit civil rights, are all expressions of causal reasoning. Due to its scientific nature, causal reasoning often relies heavily on expert testimony to establish its accuracy.

4. *Analogical Reasoning.* To draw an "analogy" is to understand one situation by showing its similarities with another situation. In everyday life, we draw analogies whenever we react to another person's experience by saying "This reminds me of the time when . . ." The constructive purpose of an analogy is to help understand one situation by drawing parallels with another, more familiar, one. This allows us to make more informed judgments by seeing what worked and what didn't in similar contexts. In rhetoric, rhetors use analogical reasoning to argue for or against actions based on their success or failure in past situations. For example, one of the most frequent analogies used to condemn American military action is that of the Vietnam War, just as the analogy used to support it is World War II. By saying "This is another Vietnam" a rhetor implies we are stuck in a quagmire, while saying "This leader is another Hitler" is to argue against any policy of appeasement. The use and effectiveness of such analogies hinge on whether the comparison is accurate and convincing.

Fallacies

Fallacies are the results of reasoning gone bad. Often called "invalid" forms of reasoning, fallacies are more accurately described as distorted forms of normal reasoning that rely on exaggeration to produce persuasive effects. Rhetoric is usually associated with "fallacious" reasoning for this purpose. Political rhetors more often than not rely on fallacies rather than more precise logic for the simple reason that public audiences find fallacies easier to understand, more interesting to hear, and more persuasive to act upon. A political scientist might reason, quite accurately, that immigration is a complex affair that offers both risks and benefits to a society, but the person who gets quoted in the news is the partisan politician who says "Either we close the border or abandon the security of our nation." Fallacies may be "invalid" from a logical standpoint, but they are often incredibly effective from a persuasive one.

Here are four of the most prevalent fallacies:

1. *Either/or.* Perhaps the most powerful of the fallacies, *either/or* presents audiences with a stark choice by presenting two clear but completely opposite alternatives. The point of *either/or* is to remove any possibility of compromise or "middle ground" by eliminating any gray area and defining the available options in black and white. Like the strategy of polarization, the intention of *either/or* is to collectively move people in a single direction by portraying one path of action in a wholly positive light while demonizing the other. These options can be described in terms of cause and effect, such as the argument that "We must either defend liberty or tyranny will reign," or in terms of competing definitional categories, such as the assertion that "You are either a patriot or a traitor." The latter example is, of course, also an example of polarization.

2. *Bandwagon.* The name for this fallacy derives from the phrase "to jump on the bandwagon." It is a form of argument that encourages an audience to do something simply because a majority of other people is doing it. Usually, however, bandwagon arguments do not appear in such blatant phrases as "Believe this because everyone else does." In advertising, bandwagon strategies are employed whenever a product is sold under the assumption that it will make one fashionable and popular. In politics, they are used whenever a principle or position is advocated because it is part of the "American spirit" or reflects the "values of the heartland," or is reflective of the "will of the people." The fallacy is that popularity does not equal legitimacy.

3. *Ad hominem.* Latin for "against the man," an *ad hominem* is an argumentative strategy that undermines opposing positions by attacking the personal character of their advocates rather than the positions themselves. *Ad hominem* attacks assault a competitor's *ethos* and by doing so make the arguments of that competitor appear to lack credibility. In political campaigns, most negative advertising takes the form of *ad hominem* fallacies, reasoning that because a candidate had an extramarital affair, lied on her taxes, or was convicted of drunk driving, then all her policy suggestions are also suspect. The fallacy is that the strength and logic of an argument on its own merits is completely separate from the character of the person who makes the argument.

4. *False cause.* The fallacy of false cause represents whenever someone disregards more sophisticated empirical methods of determining cause and effect in favor or attributing the cause to whatever person, event, or object is easily understandable to an audience and whose identification as a cause somehow benefits the rhetor. As employed in rhetoric, false causes generally fall into two categories. In the first category, the "effects" in these cases are negative ones and the "false causes" are simply things that the rhetor and the audience don't like and

find convenient to blame. Thus, the mayor of the city might blame economic decline on bad weather, a disloyal staff, or an influx of illegal immigrants. When the causes are *people*, this also goes by the name *scapegoating*. In the second category, the effects are positive and the causes are identified directly with the actions of the rhetor and his or her associates. Thus, the same mayor will then attribute subsequent success to his or her ambitious agenda, rather than weather, staff, or immigration, even in those cases when the positive effects come years after leaving office!

Emotional Appeal

Unlike reasons, which we think exist purely in the cognitive realm of language, emotions are intrinsically connected with our personal and physical states of well-being. Where reasoning reflects our capacity to think logically about abstract ideas that may be distant from our personal experience, emotions embody our tendency to feel passionately about the people, events, objects, or ideas that immediately concern us. That is to say, emotions do not simply exist as bare "feelings" that live inside our heads and bodies. They are always relational to something in our immediate environment; they are ways of interpreting, reacting, and orienting ourselves to things that stand out as significant.

The power of rhetorical discourse is often contingent upon its ability to harness of the motivational power of emotions to encourage new beliefs and actions. From a rhetorical standpoint, then, emotions can be effectively divided into ones that *attract* us to things and ones that *repel* us from them. *Attracting* emotions are ones such as love, curiosity, pity, generosity, envy, or greed. *Repelling* emotions are ones such as anger, fear, shame, cowardice, or apathy. A rhetor who wishes an audience to reject something will inspire *repelling* emotions, while *attracting* emotions will be attached to the preferred belief our course of action.

Like with good literature, however, effective rhetoric will *show* and not simply *tell*. Anyone can stand before an audience and suggest that they be angry at one thing and passionate about another. But emotions cannot simply be called forth on command. Because they are generated only in reaction to something they can tangibly experience or imagine, emotions are called forth only by rhetoric that offers rich descriptions of great and terrible things that we desire or fear. Instead of telling people to "be horrified at the brutality of the enemy," one can say "the enemy will tear out your eyes and murder your children." Instead of telling people to "feel hope for the future," one can say "we will struggle to the mountaintops to breathe in the crisp air of freedom." In the first cases the emotions are named but not called forth; in the second they are called for but not named. Rhetoric uses graphic examples to inspire emotions that make an audience turn away from one thing and toward another.

Metaphor

To use a metaphor is to define one thing by directly comparing it to something seemingly unrelated but which nonetheless shares some essential quality. To say "That man is a lion" is not to literally call him a lion but to say that he shares the qualities of ferocity and courage that we associate with lions. *Metaphor* is thus different from *analogy* because the comparison is not to be taken literally but symbolically. To argue that American democracy is similar to Greek democracy is an analogy because it implies we can learn practical lessons about governance by looking to Greek history.

By contrast, arguing that a politician is a snake is not to imply we will learn about him or her by studying snake behavior; it is simply to associate a politician with acts of deceit and manipulation.

In rhetoric, metaphors are important tools of persuasion because they are able to convey complex ideas or situations in vivid, powerful, and easily understood images. In other words, a metaphor is not simply a "window dressing" on a speech that makes it sound good; a metaphor is a way of conveying information and making arguments. Consequently, the choice of one metaphor over another often makes a significant difference in how one's rhetoric is interpreted and received. Referring to a military conflict as a "quagmire" is much different than calling it an "uphill climb," for a quagmire implies getting stuck into something from which one cannot escape while an uphill climb signifies a difficult challenge that can nonetheless be overcome with effort.

Effective rhetors take considerable effort to choose metaphors wisely so that they convey a specific meaning without unintended connotations. As a result, analyzing metaphors from a rhetorical standpoint requires great attention to detail and the ability to trace out the implications of a speaker's stylistic choices.

The Message in Performance

The message in performance is generally referred to as the *text*. Text can be used to describe a written work such as a poem, short story, or novel. But text may also be used to describe the actual live performance production. It is important to keep in mind that not all performances are constructed from or revolve around a written work. Some, like avant-garde performances, are predominantly visual in nature. Since most are familiar with and have an understanding of written literary works as texts, the focus of this section will center on the more nontraditional types of performance texts such as oral texts, action texts, and visual texts. It is important to keep in mind that these three categories are used primarily as a means of structuring this discussion. These categories are not mutually exclusive, as some overlap can and does occur. However, these categories will allow us to focus in on the predominant function or significance of each type of text.

Oral Texts

Oral texts most commonly take the form of storytelling. We discussed one type of storytelling, the *personal narrative*, in the section on agent. Personal narratives, as the term implies, are autobiographical stories which allow us to share certain events from our own lives with an audience. Another type of storytelling is family storytelling. *Family storytelling* is similar to the personal narrative in that the stories that are told are true, but instead of being autobiographical in nature, they revolve around a member of the storyteller's family. I'm sure we all have stories that we tell and retell about the time grandpa's dentures fell out while taking the family portrait or the time Aunt Sally won the blue ribbon for her pecan pie. Family stories can relate humorous happenings, proud moments, sad occasions, or embarrassing events. The telling of these stories functions to keep family history alive and serves to reinforce family identity. A third type of storytelling is the *oral history*. Oral histories function to maintain and preserve the cultural histories of particular groups of people. These groups are composed of individuals whose stories share a common thread. For example, oral histories may be collected from Holocaust survivors, victims of the 9/11 attacks, or Hurricane Katrina evacuees. The individuals from the group usually relate their respective stories to an oral historian who records and transcribes the stories for future generations.

Oral storytelling serves many purposes. The stories we tell allow us to make sense of the events that happen to us and to create some sort of order or structure in our lives. The stories also enable others to see things from our perspective. Additionally, oral storytelling offers us a way to connect with the audience on a more intimate level. The stories that we share reveal or lay bare our personal beliefs and value systems, thereby, enabling us to form a common bond with the audience who, in turn, may share in our experiences by identifying in some way with the stories that are told. Further, the stories permit us to reinforce our sense of self-worth by shaping and refashioning our personal identity. They allow us to reexamine our past, our traditions, our hardships, and our triumphs. Finally, oral stories serve not only to entertain, but to preserve our heritage and our cultural identity. Through the telling of the stories, we are able to examine and comprehend how we fit into the world around us. But, in addition to realizing our social position, we receive a clearer personal understanding of who we are, where we've come from, and where we would like to be in the future.

Action Texts

Action texts occur most frequently in the area of cultural performance. The ritual and the festival are two types of cultural performance with which you are probably most familiar. Rituals and festivals are said to contain action texts because both require activity, or a combination of participation and performance in order to exist. The text is created via the actions of the participants. A *ritual* is a customary observance or practice in which a formalized set of actions are repeated, usually in a particular setting, at regular recurring intervals. Rituals include such events as weddings, funerals, communions, and bar mitzvahs. Although rituals are often associated with an official religion or religious practice, they do not have to be religious in nature. Rituals are, however, usually related to the central core of life. In other words, rituals revolve around events related to birth, death, or some other rite of passage. Further, rituals tend to follow a fairly rigid structure of activities, meaning certain actions are performed in a certain order. For example, weddings usually begin with a processional of bridesmaids and groomsmen, followed by the bride walking down the aisle, followed by the exchanging of vows, followed by the recessional, followed by the reception. Also, as you will recall from the discussion on audience in performance, rituals contain integral audiences. This means that the audience is a necessary and functioning part of the performance. Without the audience, the ritual cannot take place. All members must actively participate in order for the ritual to occur. A festival, on the other hand, is a celebratory event centering around a particular theme, often involving some aspect of the community in which the festival occurs. Festivals are more relaxed than rituals. They include public recreational events such as Mardi Gras, rock concerts, and state fairs. And although most festivals are secular in nature, some, like Mardi Gras, may have religious roots. The structure of activities in festivals is looser or less rigid than the structure of activities in rituals. Although there may be a planned series of events within the festival, such as a schedule of balls and parades for Mardi Gras, the participants in the festival are free to pick and chose their activities, and come and go at their leisure.

Generally speaking, cultural performances like rituals and festivals take place within a community and function to bind the members of that community together. Through active participation in a common event, the performance of shared activities allows the community to build and strengthen its social relations. In addition, by engaging in the series of actions set forth by the cultural performance, the social community is able to both celebrate and reflect upon its cultural values.

Visual Texts

Visual texts in performance serve to attract attention and to stir the emotions of the audience. Two types of performance that rely heavily on visual elements are intertextual performance and avant-garde performance. *Intertextual* performance features the interplay of texts. Intertextuality can be accomplished in two basic ways. The first is by referencing one or more secondary texts within the primary text. The *Shrek* movies are wonderful examples of this type of intertextuality. Within the main texts of *Shrek* and *Shrek 2* are references to other texts such as *Pinocchio*, *The Three Little Pigs*, and *The Gingerbread Man*. Further, the *Shrek* films incorporate references to TV shows such as *Cops* and other popular films like *The Matrix*. A specific example of an intertextual moment occurs in the final scene of *Shrek 2*. Puss In Boots and Donkey are singing and dancing onstage. At one point in his dance, Puss leans back in a chair, pulls a chain, and is hit by a deluge of water from above. This scene is a reference to the Jennifer Beals scene in the 1983 film, *Flashdance*. Of course, to fully appreciate intertextuality of this nature, the audience must be familiar with the secondary text being referenced. The sight of a cat being hit by a flood of water may be a funny in and of itself; however, an additional level of humor arises from the awareness of the interplay of the two texts.

The second way to accomplish intertextuality is to combine two or more existing primary texts. The new meaning that is created through the juxtaposition of these texts serves to question, subvert, or challenge the dominant ideology inherent within the texts themselves. For example, Adel Comeaux used an intertextual performance to call into question our cultural idea of beauty. She felt that society places too much emphasis on external appearance as opposed to internal beauty. For her performance, she combined film clips from *Shallow Hal*, *The Princess Diaries*, and *The Little Mermaid*. These clips featured women whose appearance had been changed from fat to thin, awkward to graceful, and beautiful to ugly. The performance also included footage from the Dove ad, "How Real Beauty is Made." This footage showed a model's face being digitally enhanced to appear even more appealing. Along with the images of externally beautiful women, Adel juxtaposed a photograph of Mother Theresa. Although Mother Theresa may not be considered a "beauty" by society's standards, her inner nature made her a beautiful woman. Finally, the song "I Feel Pretty" from *West Side Story* was used as musical accompaniment for the visual texts. Adel wanted the audience to consider whether or not outer appearance always mirrored inner appearance, thus she titled her intertextual performance, *Mirror Mirror*.

With intertextuality, the performer *makes* meaning instead of discovering meaning by questioning, parodying, or critiquing existing works. Intertextuality permits the texts to "speak" with one another. These texts do not relinquish their individuality, but allow for comparisons to be made between them. When the texts are perceived together in a single performance, the range of impressions and meanings expands.

Avant-garde is a rebellious type of performance that intentionally rejects conventional aesthetic conventions. Avant-garde performers strive to be significantly different by shocking, provoking, or disturbing the audience in some way. The avant-garde performer, or performance artist, may use elements of the body, such as voice, gesture, and movement, to turn their own bodies into works of art. This type of avant-garde performance is known as body art. One example of body art is living sculptures where performers position themselves on street corners or other public areas. Other performance artists rely on multimedia techniques, incorporating moving images and sound into the performance. Regardless of the actual content, all avant-garde performances are nonrepresentational and visually powerful. Avant-garde performers use visual elements to attract attention and stir emotions in a number of different ways. First, a performer may use a familiar object in an unfamiliar way. This technique is known as *defamiliarizing the familiar*. For example, the performer may use a hairbrush to brush his or her teeth, or use condiments such as ketchup, mustard, and mayonnaise in place of lipstick, eyeshadow, and blush. Second, a performer may incorporate *contrast*. The contrast can involve color, music, movement, or emotion. One avant-garde performer played a soft, soothing lullaby while violently struggling to free himself from ropes binding his wrists and ankles. A third technique that is used by avant-garde performers is *repetition*. Repetition involves the repeating of a sound, word, phrase, or movement throughout the performance. During one particular avant-garde performance, the performer wrapped herself in a strand of blinking Christmas lights while a tape-recorded voice repeated the words, "What do you want? I don't know. What do you want? I don't know." Finally, a performer may use the technique of *incongruity* where a series of actions or visuals are presented, one after the other, but seem to have no relevant connection to each other. For example, a performer may walk on stage, open an umbrella, eat an apple, sweep the floor, blow his nose into a handkerchief, and walk off the stage.

Visual texts in performance serve to get, control, and focus the audience's attention. The visual elements allow the performer to fashion "reality" in the way he or she wishes the audience to see it. Both intertextual and avant-garde performances challenge the audience to become actively engaged by becoming critical viewers of the visual texts.

Message Exercises

Symbol Exercise #1: Communication Theory

1. Walk through a student parking lot. Make a note of the kinds of stickers and decals on student vehicles. What do you "learn" about the owners based on these physical objects? Now walk through a faculty/staff parking lot. Make a note of the kinds of stickers and decals on these vehicles. What do you "learn" about the owners based on these physical objects? In what ways are these similar or different from the ones you saw in the student lot?

Symbol Exercise #2: Communication Theory

2. Look through your favorite magazine or Web site. Find at least three pictures that reflect something you like or desire. This thing does not have to be a physical object. The picture may reflect affluence or power or some other abstract concept. In groups of 3, share your pictures. Without discussion, each person should look at the other 2 people's pictures and make a list of what you "read" in the picture. After you have your lists, compare your lists of what you think the pictures represent. In what ways did you agree? In what ways did you disagree?

Language Exercise #1: Communication Theory

1. Make a list of 10 categories that reflect groups of people. The groups should not be based on sex, race, or ethnicity. For example, you might include athletes or soccer players, but not football players. For each group, identify at least one term for that group that would be considered a compliment and one that would be considered an insult. Speculate on how these words have the ability to praise or hurt.

Language Exercise #2: Communication Theory

2. In the exercise on the self, you listed words that describe you. Go back and look at that list. Pick one word from the list that describes something you like about yourself and one word that describes something that you don't like about yourself. Think of a word that has the opposite meaning. For example, if you listed "smart" as a quality you possess, an alternative might be "stupid." Discuss what it means to you to "have" the quality of the word you think describes you and to "not have" the quality of the opposite word. For the example, how is it different being "smart" versus "not being stupid"? Re-evaluate the words you used to describe you. Do they reflect you as well as the words that are their opposites? Why or why not?

Nonverbal Exercise #1: Communication Theory

1. Walk through a public space on campus (the quad, student union, library, etc.). Observe groups of at least 2 people in this public space. Note their use of space, touch, eye contact, etc. How do you know that these people are "together"? What kind of relationship do you think these people have? How can you tell?

Nonverbal Exercise #2: Communication Theory

2. Nonverbal messages are used to share emotions. Look through magazines and newspapers to find pictures that reflect a range of emotions. Bring at least 3 pictures into class. Share your pictures with at least 3 other people. Each person should indicate what emotion they think the picture reflects without discussing it among yourselves. Once everyone has identified the emotions for each picture, compare your lists. Do you agree or disagree on the emotion being represented? What do you see in the picture that led you to your selection?

Reasoning Exercise #1: Rhetoric

1. As a class, come up with a fanciful problem that needs to be explained and then justified through the process of reasoning. (For example, "Why did the chicken cross the road?") Assign ONE form of reasoning to each member of the class. Each student will then come up with an answer to the question using their form of reasoning to provide a justification for their answer. (This exercise can then be expanded with the first exercise of Fallacies.)

Reasoning Exercise #2: Rhetoric

2. Read a recent newspaper article that deals with some public controversy. Read it thoroughly and identify all the quotes or explanations that either raise a question of reasoning or rely on some form of reasoning to explain or justify a position. Then offer your analysis as to how strong these reasons are in a rhetorical sense.

Fallacies Exercise #1: Rhetoric

1. After going through Exercise #1 in Reasoning, now assign a fallacy to each student and have them attempt to "refute" another student's explanation using a fallacious argument. Make sure to "pair up" two students to refute each other so as to create a "debate" atmosphere.

Fallacies Exercise #2: Rhetoric

2. Find a print advertisement that you feel relies on a fallacy to sell its product. Analyze the purpose of the ad and describe how the implied or explicit fallacy it contains aids in this purpose.

Emotion Exercise #1: Rhetoric

1. Create a list of attracting and repelling emotions on the board that function as "pairs" in the sense of being opposites. (For example, love and hate, cowardice and courage, etc.) Number these pairs and have the instructor write them down on pieces of paper. Distribute these numbers to each student without letting the class know what numbers have been assigned. Each student must now write a description of some scene, event, person, or action that embodies both of these emotions WITHOUT naming ANY emotion or using the word "feel." (For example, to describe "love" you might say "my heart started beating wildly when I saw him/her") Give this description in front of class and see if they can identify the emotions you attempted to show.

Emotion Exercise #2: Rhetoric

2. Find an example from literary fiction that you believe powerfully shows an emotional response to something that has rhetorical implications. Copy the example and describe the emotion you believe it shows, making sure to pinpoint particular phrases or images or ideas that you connect with that emotion.

Metaphor Exercise #1: Rhetoric

1. As a class, come up a "quality" of an action or an event that you wish to describe, such as an "intelligent" action or a "terrible" event. Come up with 5 different metaphors to describe this thing. Then list 3 implications for each metaphor that are UNIQUE to that metaphor in the sense that they are not included in any of the other metaphors. After doing this, select which you think is the best metaphor to use if you were a political rhetor praising or condemning this thing.

Metaphor Exercise #2: Rhetoric

2. Effective political cartoons are often based on employing metaphors to represent public issues. Find a political cartoon that uses a metaphor, describe its metaphorical function, give 5 implications of that metaphor, and then show what practical consequences it might have as a rhetorical act.

Orality Exercise #1: Performance

1. Names give us a sense of personal identity as well as family identity. Some family names are passed down from generation to generation. Others are uniquely invented or created for that specific individual. Tell the story of how you received your name (or nickname). How has your name affected your self-concept? How has it reinforced your family identity?

Orality Exercise #2: Performance

2. Family stories function to keep family history alive. Tell the story of a humorous or embarrassing moment involving a member of your family. Is this story told often by other family members? At what occasions is the story told? Who usually tells the story? Why do you think the story is told and re-told? What purpose does it serve in your family?

Action Text Exercise #1: Performance

1. Describe something that you do, or take part in, that you would consider to be a ritual. What is the order of prescribed activities for this ritual? What personal and cultural values do you believe this ritual upholds?

Action Text Exercise #2: Performance

2. Attend a festival such as Fall Fest, Jazz Fest, Fest for All, or the Strawberry Festival and answer the following questions:

   a. Which activities did you take part in?

   b. What was the overall tone of the event?

   c. What is the significance of this festival to the community? What community values does it uphold?

Visual Text Exercise #1: Performance

1. Both parodies and metaphors contain elements of intertextuality. A parody is a humorous imitation of another, usually more serious, work. It draws its humor from imitating some element or elements from the original work, yet exaggerating or distorting those elements in some way. The *Scary Movie* films, for example, are parodies of familiar horror films. A metaphor compares one thing in terms of another. Unlike parodies, metaphors are not necessarily humorous. For instance, print ads for Murray's Sugar-Free Cookies compare other sugar-free cookies to pieces of corrugated cardboard.

For this exercise find (or create) a visual example of parody or metaphor. Turn in this example along with your answers to the following questions:

a. What original work is being parodied? OR What is being used as a metaphor for what?

b. What is the general purpose of the parody? What comment is being made through the use of parody? OR What is the significance of the metaphor? What point is being made?

Visual Text Exercise #2: Performance

2. Choose two contrasting words, such as "love and hate," "joy and sorrow," or "hot and cold." Combine these words into a visual image that creates new meaning through the juxtaposition of these words.

Visual Text Exercise #3: Performance

3. Choose an object. Create a still, visual performance in which you use that object or item to signify both "life" and "death."

Section 4

Meaning

Meaning in communication refers generally to the "content" of the message as interpreted by both the agent and the audience.

Meaning in Communication Theory

For communication theorists, meaning does not lie in the message, but in the people exchanging the message. ***Meaning*** is negotiated through cultural, social, and interpersonal constraints, therefore the interpretation of messages depends on situational factors. As was discussed in the section on ***messages***, *symbols* are arbitrary and ambiguous. The meaning assigned to a symbol is a social process that is filtered through personal experience. As we talked about in the section on the ***agent***, perception plays a role in how we see the world and our place in it. Thus, meaning depends on how we interpret the messages we receive.

Interpretation

Interpretation is the assigning of meaning to the things that we perceive in our world. How we interpret messages depends on the possible meanings that can be assigned to a symbol, the place of a single message within an array of other messages, and the situation in which we receive the message. As was discussed in the section on ***symbols***, symbols are arbitrary and ambiguous. The meaning of a symbol is not inherent in the symbol itself, but is agreed upon by the social group. Because the social group assigns meaning, meaning can change over time or from one group to another. Ambiguity in symbols comes from many sources and results in the potential for multiple meanings being assigned to the same symbol.

Denotative and Connotative Meanings

Social groups agree on the meaning that is to be assigned a word or action; however, complete agreement on the meaning does not exist. The meaning of a word or an action has more than one level. We refer to one level of meaning as *denotative* or the dictionary (direct, explicit) definition of a word. This definition is the social group's formally agreed upon definition of a word, so that "cat" means cat and "dog" means dog. We can also refer to the *connotative* (implied or suggested) meaning of a word. For example, when we mention the word dog, one person may think of a favorite pet from childhood and another thinks of the dog that bit her when she was a child. Thus, the connotative meaning reflects what we associate with or how we evaluate the thing that is represented by the word;

often this is an emotional response. These differences in connotative meaning can lead to misunderstandings because we might be talking about the same "thing," but feel differently about that thing.

Content and Relational Levels of Meaning

Most of the messages that we receive do not occur in isolation from other messages, especially during face-to-face interactions. The meaning that is assigned to a string of words in any given utterance depends on accompanying messages. In the section on ***messages***, we discussed verbal and nonverbal messages. Verbal messages convey the content level of meaning while nonverbal messages convey the relational level of meaning. The *content level* of a message consists of the words that are spoken or written. First, we assign meaning based on the linguistic content, that is, the words themselves and their grammatical relationship to one another. The content level of meaning is relatively objective in that anyone who speaks the language would say "these words mean this . . . ." The *relational level* of a message depends on how those words are spoken, who says them, and in what situation. The relational level of meaning is more subjective in that any two people may assign different meanings to the same set of words based on what other factors they take into consideration in making their interpretations. These differences can result in misunderstandings to which a common response is: "That's not what I meant!"

The words "I love you, too!" on the content level mean that the speaker is sharing an emotion in response to another person's behavior. The relational meaning that you assign to these words depends on the situation. If you just said "I love you," then these words being spoken in a soft tone and accompanied by a caress are likely to be assigned the meaning that the other person does, indeed, feel the same emotions towards you that you feel towards him or her. If, however, these words are spoken with a note of sarcasm by a person to whom you have just been rude, you might assume that this person does not really love you, but is making a snide comment about your behavior. We tend to believe the nonverbal cues that accompany a spoken message and assign meaning accordingly. Remember in the section on verbal and nonverbal messages, we discussed how nonverbal messages can emphasize or contradict verbal messages. Because nonverbal messages transmit emotion, we tend to believe the nonverbal message more than the verbal one. You can say anything, but your actions speak louder than words!

Situational Constraints

As was discussed in the section on audience, *situational constraints* exist on many levels and include what is said, what else has been said, who is speaking, and the situation in which the exchange takes place. Each of these elements of the situation provides us with clues about how to interpret a message. What is said includes the content of the message as well as the way in which it was said, as we discussed in the section on content and relational levels of meaning. The meaning we assign is also influenced by what else has been said. The phrase "he's a nut" could take on several meanings, depending on to whom "he" refers and what else has been said about "him." Who makes the statement influences how we interpret a message. For example, "You sure look nice today" from a friend would probably be considered a nice compliment. However, if a boss says this to a subordinate, it might be considered to be sexual harassment. Finally, the social situation influences how a message is interpreted. Talking to your friend about your custody battle might be appropriate and helpful at home, but probably not so appropriate at a wedding reception.

Shared Meaning

We use words to share our sense of the world with others. An important element of personal and social relationships is the development of shared meaning. *Shared meaning* reflects similar interpretations by the parties involved. A goal in many relationships is to be really understood by the other person, whether that person is a friend, a family member, or a coworker. We transfer our experience into symbols in ways to share that experience with others. Most of the time we follow relatively scripted interactions. We may, however, be very strategic in the way we phrase our words, our nonverbal behavior as we make a statement, and our selection of the time and place to say the words. We generally reserve these very strategic choices for times of great importance. For example, when interacting with your boss on a regular basis, you may exchange pleasantries and discuss what needs to be accomplished during the course of the day in fairly routine ways. When you want to ask for a raise, however, you may decide to dress more neatly, schedule an appointment so that you will not be interrupted, and practice how to impress upon your boss how much you have contributed to the organization.

Assigning meaning to any message is a complex process due to the arbitrary and ambiguous nature of symbols, the personal characteristics of the agent, the personal characteristics of the audience, the relationship between the agent and the audience, and the context within which the exchange is taking place. When you think about all the things that can go wrong, it's amazing to think about how often we actually do manage to understand one another!

Meaning in Rhetoric

The *meaning* of rhetorical discourse is located not in words but in practice. Because rhetoric is oriented toward social action, the *practical* meaning of rhetoric is determined by the effects it has on audiences and their subsequent decisions and attitudes. There is, of course, also a textual meaning located in the discourse itself that we can interpret much as we would do with a poem or a tract of philosophy. Much of what is called *rhetorical criticism* engages in this aspect of interpretation that is detached from questions of practical effect. However, the final judgment of any rhetorical act is ultimately how it impacts the social world in which we live. Without starting with this practical meaning, rhetoric becomes indistinguishable from any other form of communication.

Exigence

A rhetorical *exigence* represents a practical problem that has the capacity to be resolved, at least in part, through rhetorical persuasion. That is to say, problems that do not require rhetorical intervention, such as the act of fixing a flat tire, are not rhetorical exigencies. However, fixing a flat tire may *become* a rhetorical exigence when you cannot do it on your own and must persuade someone driving by to help you. The key characteristic of a *rhetorical* exigence is that successful resolution of the problem requires action by an audience not already predisposed to act. Thus, asking someone for a drink of water is not usually a rhetorical exigence because people are more than willing to oblige in normal circumstances. However, a person being held hostage may have to employ all their rhetorical powers to appeal to the humanity of their captors and resolve the exigence of being starving or dying of thirst.

Most exigencies are not so clear-cut as this example, however. In fact, often the rhetorical debate revolves around whether one's characterization of an exigency is accurate, or whether it even exists at all. Is America in moral decline? Is a fetus a human being? Does global warming exist? Does gay marriage threaten traditional values? For many groups, the challenge is not to solve a problem but to raise and define one. Consequently, it is helpful to distinguish between a *contested* and an *uncontested* exigence.

A *contested* exigence is not universally accepted by an audience as real, and hence the rhetorical debate surrounds the existence rather than the solution to a problem. For example, a small minority of people still believe that the world will end in the near future and spend their energy convincing others of their impending doom. While they feel passionately that this exists as a problem, the majority of people dismiss them as crazy. By contrast, an *uncontested* exigence is a universally accepted problem whose solution remains in debate. The struggle to eradicate poverty is a longstanding exigence to which people offer competing solutions, most of which fail to rally a consensus for the sake of action. That is to say, to acknowledge a problem is not necessarily to have the means or even the will to solve it.

Because rhetoric is only meaningful *as* rhetoric within the world of practice, its analysis is incomplete without an account of the exigencies that are defined or addressed through persuasive discourse. It is in this sense that advertising, while clearly a means of persuasion, is not correctly classified as rhetorical discourse. Advertising is simply a means of earning a profit by creating a sense of desire for one's product. While in some cases products are seen as a means to solving actual problems (like the common claims of foods to be "heart healthy" or "fat free" in response to the public exigencies of heart disease and obesity) in general these problems are themselves only exploited to sell more products. Rhetoric, by contrast, addresses public problems through a kind of persuasive discourse that addresses the problems directly by appeal to collective public action.

Judgment

Once a rhetorical exigence is defined, the challenge to a rhetor is to advance a form of judgment appropriate for that exigence. A *judgment* is the act of defining a particular person, object, or event in terms of a general category for the purposes of making a practical decision. It thus involves the relationship between a *thing*, an *idea*, and an *action*. Using a nonrhetorical example, I wake up at night and here a tapping sound (thing). Fearful that it is a burglar (initial idea), I get up and discover it is just the rattling of the air conditioner (conclusive idea). I then decide to go back to sleep (action). We make hundreds of such judgments every day without realizing it because they have become habitual. But any parent realizes how such a simple thing as a tapping sound can represent any number of terrors to a young child. Because they have not developed habits of judgment, they cannot distinguish the sound of thunder from the sound of a creature under their bed. Thus, a major part of our educational process is the cultivation of a common judgment so that individuals all use the same ideas to classify the same things and thus behave in common ways.

Rhetoric, however, is not concerned with such habitual judgments that are simply part of our everyday life. Rather, they are concerned with situations where the proper judgment about a thing is uncertain and contingent. Is the new boyfriend of your daughter a "gentleman" or a "little punk"? Rhetorical conflict arises when you think the latter and your daughter attempts to persuade you of the former. Of course, in a social controversy the stakes are much broader. Is a foreign power an "ally" or an "enemy"? Is capital punishment a "necessary deterrent to crime" or a "violation of human rights"? Is the melting of a glacier a sign of "global warming" or simply a "natural fluctuation of temperature"? Rhetorical conflict involves the struggle to advance one judgment over another and thereby encourage forms of action on the basis of that judgment.

In other words, rhetorical exigencies require us first to make a judgment about the nature of the problem (thereby translating a contested exigence into an uncontested one), and then to make a judgment about the nature of the solution (thereby translating uncertainty into action). Rhetorical analysis requires us to be able to identify the judgments that are encouraged by a rhetor and then to decide on the wisdom and efficacy of such judgments.

Social Knowledge

The goal of rhetoric within democratic deliberation is the establishment or modification of *social knowledge*, which stands for the generally accepted conventions, attitudes, and values of a community. In this sense, *social knowledge* represents the collective judgments of a social group that are the result of past experience and which guide beliefs and behaviors in future situations. For example, the horrors of World War II taught many nations the lesson that one should not appease dictators or turn a blind eye to gross violations of human rights. These lessons are now part of our social knowledge that we use to justify military intervention against totalitarian states that pursue genocidal policies. They are commonly held judgments about past events that influence the decision we make about present conflicts.

Rhetoric both draws from the pool of social knowledge to justify actions as well as helps create social knowledge in response to new situations. In the first case, a rhetor draws from available social knowledge to authorize a similar action in the present. For example, social knowledge concerning racial inequality was long used to justify particular acts of segregation, as Governor Wallace demonstrated when he protested the integration of Alabama schools by declaring "Segregation forever!" In the second case, a rhetor responds to a conflict by advancing a novel judgment that attempts to modify or replace some aspect of social knowledge using the strength of persuasion. Martin Luther King Jr. attempted to change social attitudes about race relations through his rhetoric, and because he challenged established conventions his orations were considered radical at the time they were given. However, over the years they contributed to a collective shift in public attitudes to the extent that his speeches are now used to promote social knowledge concerning the inherent dignity and equality of all human beings.

The meaning of a particular rhetorical act is thus ultimately determined by its impact on social knowledge, by how it affects the collective judgments of a population. These impacts are *immediate* and *long term*. *Immediate* impacts are determined by the direct effects a speech has on its audience in a specific time and place and in response to a particular situation. Most rhetoric is generally confined to these immediate impacts as situations change quickly and people move on to new challenges. However, great speeches often have *long-term* impacts because they influence people across great expanses of space and time. Lincoln's Gettysburg Address was initially delivered to give a boost to the Union troops during a critical time of the Civil War; but it has come to stand for one of the greatest expressions of the meaning of American democracy.

It is important when studying historical speeches that one does not judge success or failure only by the standards of immediate impacts. To do so blinds us to the long-term significance that rhetoric has on constituting the social knowledge of a culture.

Meaning in Performance

As we learned previously, performers perform in order to recreate reality in the way they wish the audience to see it. Whether performing an everyday role, offering an interpretation of a literary text, telling a personal story, celebrating a ritual, or creating an avant-garde work, all performances contain meaning. *Meaning* refers to that which is expressed by the performance, or the overall significance of the performance itself.

There are several types of meaning in the area of performance, including intentional meaning, perceived meaning, objective meaning, symbolic meaning, and emotional meaning. It is easier to understand and distinguish between these types of meanings if we applying them to a specific example. For this example, I will use an avant-garde performance presented by Christian Wolf. Christian began his performance by draping a bright red tablecloth over a table. He placed a small, wooden crate beside the table. He reached into the crate with his left hand and pulled out an egg. He gently placed the egg on the center of the red tablecloth. He then raised his right hand. In this hand he held a large mallet. He swiftly brought the mallet down on top of the egg, splattering the contents across the table, into the audience, and onto the floor. He repeated this series of actions twelve times. When he placed his hand inside the wooden crate for the thirteenth time, he pulled out a live baby chicken. He placed the chicken in the same spot as the smashed eggs, raised the mallet, swiftly let it drop, but stopped right before it made contact with the living chick.

Now let us explore the various meanings within this particular performance event. The first is *intentional meaning.* Intentional meaning refers to the fixed aim or purpose of the performer. When creating or structuring a performance, the performer has a specific goal in mind, whether it be to criticize the war in Iraq, comment upon the hazards of smoking, or shed light on the nation's problem with obesity. In his performance, Christian wanted to express his negative attitude and feelings against abortion. Christian used the eggs to represent the unborn fetuses, the smashing action of the mallet to represent the act of abortion, and the live baby chicken to represent the living baby. The second type of meaning is *perceived meaning.* Perceived meaning is the audience's interpretation or understanding of the performance. The perceived meaning may or may not be the same as the performer's intended meaning. As we learned in communication theory, perception varies from individual to individual. Because we are each influenced by our different experiences, we will assign meaning based on those experiences. Many in the audience may have interpreted Christian's performance as an anti-abortion piece. However, there may have been a practicing vegan in the audience who understood Christian's performance as speaking out against eating chicken and eggs. Still, others may have viewed the performance as a protest against factory farms and the inhumane treatment of the animals who are raised there. Although every performance will contain an intended meaning created by the performer, every performance will also contain a perceived meaning, which may be beyond the performer's control.

Performances contain objective, symbolic, and emotional meaning as well. The *objective meaning* deals with the external facts of the performance. It is similar to communication theory's denotative meaning. In other words, it is the generally agreed upon meaning of what literally occurred in the performance. Most in the audience could agree that Christian placed eggs, one by one, in the center of a red table cloth and smashed them with a mallet. They could also agree that Christian placed a live baby chick on the table cloth, raised the mallet to hit the chick, but stopped just short of making contact.

The *symbolic meaning* is the figurative or metaphorical meaning. Actions, objects, colors, or images used by the performer within the performance may be used to signify or represent other things. In his performance, Christian used the red table cloth to symbolize bloodshed and the eggs to symbolize growing fetuses. The mallet was used to represent those who perform abortions, while the smashing action represented the killing of the fetuses. The live chicken was used as a metaphor for the living baby. The baby chick signified what the egg could become if allowed to develop, and, in turn, symbolized the aborted fetus who could have become a living child. The action of stopping the mallet just short of crushing the chick represented the halting of the abortion. Although the performer may intentionally use actions and objects to symbolize other things, the symbolic meaning must also be interpreted by the audience. Thus, what the audience perceives may be different from what the performer intended. For example, Christian intended the smashing action of the mallet to symbolize the act of abortion: however, an audience member may have interpreted that action as symbolic of the cruel killing of animals in factory farms.

The *emotional meaning* refers to the feelings, sentiments, or attitudes expressed by the viewing audience. Christian's performance elicited various emotional responses from the audience. There were many "oohs" and "aahs" vocally expressed at the sight of the cute baby chick. However, these warm, fuzzy expressions were replaced with gasps of horror when Christian raised the mallet over the baby chick. Many in the audience closed their eyes so they would not be confronted with the aftermath of the death of the baby chick. When Christian stopped his hand before making contact with the chick, many breathed an audible sigh of relief. Emotional meaning can vary among individuals within the audience. Some who viewed Christian's performance had feelings of pity for the baby chick, others were shocked to see a live baby chicken in a performance, and still others found the performance grotesquely amusing.

All performances have an intended meaning created by the performer and a perceived meaning interpreted by the audience. In addition, performances contain an objective meaning which can be agreed upon by most in the audience, and an emotional meaning which may vary from individual to individual. Finally, some performances contain symbolic meaning which is designed by the performer, but must be interpreted by the audience. The range of meanings for a given performance may be fairly narrow or may vary greatly depending upon the nature of the performance itself. In most traditional literary performances, personal narratives, family storytelling and ethnographic performances, the gap between the objective meaning and the symbolic meaning is very small. Therefore, these types of performances lend themselves to similar interpretations among members of the audience. Rituals have a larger gap between objective and symbolic meaning, but the interpretation of the symbolic meaning is usually the same for all audience members. For example, the symbolic act of exchanging rings during a wedding ceremony will be interpreted by the guests as symbolizing the love and commitment of the bride and groom. Likewise, the drinking of the grape juice or wine during communion symbolizes receiving the blood of Christ for the members of the congregation. Avant-garde performances, on the other hand, have the largest gap between objective and symbolic meaning These performances do not imitate or mirror an objective reality because the actions or objects within these performances do not convey one absolute meaning, but multiple meanings. Thus, as demonstrated by Christian's performance, the recreated reality may and should have different meanings for different individuals.

Meaning Exercises

Interpretation Exercise #1: Communication Theory

1. As a class, make a list of six or seven words, starting with fairly concrete terms (e.g., car, desert) and moving to more abstract terms (e.g., patriotism, love). For each word, each individual should write down the denotative and connotative meanings. Compare your list to at least one other person in class. In what ways did your meanings agree and disagree?

denotative meaning	**connotative meaning**

Interpretation Exercise #2: Communication Theory

2. With a partner, practice the dialogue below.

Person A: Hi

Person B: What's up

Person A: Not much

Person B: Really

Now, repeat the dialogue, but think about how you would express yourself if you are strangers waiting for the first day of class to start.

Repeat the dialogue again, but this time, think about how you would express yourself if you are roommates and Person B knows that Person A is late paying his or her share of the rent.

Once more, repeat the dialogue. This time think about how you would express yourself if you are romantic partners and Person B knows that Person A wants to avoid talking about the fight you had yesterday.

How did you vary the use of nonverbals to reflect these different situations?

Shared Meaning Exercise #1: Communication Theory

1. Watch a television show or a movie with a friend. Afterwards, talk about what you liked and disliked about the show or movie. Did you like and dislike the same or different elements of the show or movie? Did your opinion change after the two of you had talked? What did your friend point out about the show or movie that changed your opinion?

Shared Meaning Exercise #2: Communication Theory

2. Look through magazines and newspapers and find a picture that you like. Write down what it is that you like about the picture. Bring your picture to class. Share it with one other person who will share his or her picture with you. Write down what you like about his or her picture. Discuss how you saw the pictures in similar and different ways and what you learned about the other person through this discussion.

Exigence Exercise #1: Rhetoric

1. Go online and find a blog or Internet discussion board where different people has posted arguments concerning the status of some social problem—specifically dealing with whether or not it exists, and if it does, its causes and consequences. Copy three different entries that convey different opinions and analyze their claims and the forms of reasoning they employ to make their case.

Exigence Exercise #2: Rhetoric

2. Outside of class, ask 15 people to identify a contested exigence—some social problem that the public has not fully recognized as a problem—they feel needs recognition. Copy them down. Then choose one of these, give a concrete example that you feel graphically demonstrates the problem, and then portray a hypothetical negative consequence in the future that you feel will happen should the exigence not be resolved.

Judgment Exercise #1: Rhetoric

1. Find a "hard news" article in a national newspaper that deals with the political analysis of some social controversy. Copy down two quotes that show competing judgments about the same event, object, person, or issue. Explicitly label the object of judgment, the two different categories being applied to that object, and the practical consequences that follow from each category if applied.

Judgment Exercise #2: Rhetoric

2. Now take a common object (and only an object) in your immediate environment that is familiar to the class and to which they all probably hold the same attitude. Now pass a new judgment on this object that intends to change those attitudes, generally by trying to turn something "good" into something "bad," or vice versa. (However, make sure the category you apply is more specific than "good" or "bad.") Like Exercise 1, label the object, category, and consequences.

Social Knowledge Exercise #1: Rhetoric

1. Read a presidential inaugural address provided by your instructor. Print it out, read it closely, and underline every phrase that you think appeals to some aspect of social knowledge, even if it is simply a cliché or maxim or commonplace. Then take one of those passages and state more clearly why you think it appeals to social knowledge, identify that social knowledge, hypothesize its origins, and then determine the kinds of impact it is supposed to have in the context of the speech.

Social Knowledge Exercise #2: Rhetoric

2. Rhetoric deals not only with appealing to social knowledge, but changing it as new events challenge old ideas. As a class, come up with three recent major events that have had national significance in terms of how we think of ourselves as a nation. Choose one of these events and explain how it may have challenged old beliefs and values as well as how it could be used rhetorically to create new ones.

Meaning Exercise #1: Performance

1. Select a particular image or word. Explain the objective, symbolic, and emotional meanings contained within that image or word.

Meaning Exercise #2: Performance

2. Bring to class one object (or photo of the object) that you consider to be "good" and one object (or photo of the object) that you consider to be "bad." You will be asked to display these objects (or photos) for the class. Discussion will follow.

Meaning Exercise #3: Performance

3. Stage "red." Describe below what kind of meanings you intend to convey and how the performance will convey them.

Meaning Exercise #4: Performance

4. Personal perception is influenced by many factors. Perception can be affected by biological influences such as the senses, age, sex and gender, health, and temporal cycles such as fatigue, hunger, and mood. It can also be affected by personal influences like self-concept, homophily, past experiences, personal prototypes, and personal attitude systems. Finally, perception can be affected by such sociocultural influences as occupation, economic factors, race, ethnicity, or nationality, geographic or regional factors, and the media or popular culture.

For this activity, you will be given an index card containing a particular word. You are to locate three visual images that, according to your perception, reflect the meaning of this word to you. In three substantial or "meaty" paragraphs, one for each image, explain why you feel each image represents this particular word. Your explanation should include references to the specific biological, personal, or sociocultural influences that impacted your selection of each image.